TELEVISION AND RELIGION

TELEVISION AND RELIGION

THE SHAPING OF FAITH, VALUES, AND CULTURE

WILLIAM F. FORE

AUGSBURG Publishing House

TELEVISION AND RELIGION
The Shaping of Faith, Values, and Culture

Scripture quotations unless otherwise noted are from the Revised Standard Version of the Bible, copyright 1946, 1952, and 1971 by the Division of Christian Education of the National Council of Churches.

Scripture quotations designated NEB are from the New English Bible, copyright © The Delegates of the Oxford University Press and The Syndics of the Cambridge University Press, 1961, 1970, reprinted by permission.

Citations from the following articles by William Fore published in *The Christian Century* are copyright Christian Century Foundation and are used by permission:
  "Mass Media's Mythic World: At Odds with Christian Values," January 19, 1977, pp. 32-38;
  "A Critical Eye on Televangelism," September 23, 1981, pp. 939-941;
  "Beyond the Electronic Church," January 7-14, 1981, pp. 29-30;
  "Religion and Television: Report on the Research," July 18-24, 1984, pp. 710-713;
  "Media Violence: Hazardous to Our Health," September 25, 1985, pp. 834-836;
  "A New World Order in Communication," April 14, 1982, pp. 442-446.

Citations from the following articles by William Fore published in *Christianity and Crisis*, 537 W. 121st Street, New York, NY 10027, are used with permission:
  "Media and Democracy," May 17, 1971, pp. 94-98;
  "A Manual for the People: Deprogramming Television," May 2, 1977, pp. 93-96.

Citations from William Fore, "Communication and Religion in the Technological Era," in *The Myth of the Information Revolution*, edited by Michael Traber (Newbury Park, Calif.: Sage, 1986), pp. 126-137, are used by permission of the publisher.

Library of Congress Cataloging-in-Publication Data

Fore, William F.
  TELEVISION AND RELIGION.

  Bibliography: p.
  Includes index.
  1. Television in religion.   I. Title.
BV656.3.F67   1987   260   87-1214
ISBN 0-8066-2268-7

Manufactured in the U.S.A.   APH 10-6229

          3   4   5   6   7   8   9   0   1   2   3   4   5   6   7   8   9

To my parents

Frank K. Fore
Willie C. Fore

who taught me the importance
of communication and community.

CONTENTS

PREFACE

Mine was the last generation before television. TV arrived on the scene shortly after World War II, which was when I graduated from high school. Like Woody Allen, I remember a time when *there was no TV.*

But in 1952, while television was still in its infancy and I was still in seminary, I began to write, direct, and produce a program for children on New Haven's only TV station. In those simpler days you could do it all, and I wrote a weekly TV script for two years, made the sets, rehearsed one day every week, and even functioned as technical director, blocking out camera angles and shots. The program went out live, every Saturday, right after "The Singing Chef." It was called "Exploring God's World," and we got more cards and letters than all the other programs on the station combined. This led to a stint as a consultant at CBS on a summer program for children. But then I moved back to church communications where, for 30 years, I have worked in daily contact with friends and colleagues in the world of broadcasting and film, but on behalf of the world of religion.

I relate this history because the tension between these two worlds—broadcasting and religion—has been a focal point in my life. Out of this experience I have come to realize that this same tension with which I have had to deal is, in a larger sense, at the center of the question of what we—you and I and our children—can be today and will become tomorrow. I have come to believe that religion and television are the symbols and in many ways the concrete embodiments of the powers that are contending for our very souls.

The thesis of this book is that today television is beginning to usurp a role which until recently has been the role of the church in our society, namely, to shape our system of values, embody our faith, and express our cultural essence. This shift, from a religious center to what I call a technological center, is ominous. It represents a shift from dealing with human questions to dealing instead with utilitarian questions, from asking, How will this affect people? to asking only, How will this make a profit? The shift is not yet irreversible, but it soon will be if viewers do not begin to recognize the problem and learn how to cope with television in ways which allow them to accept its benefits without succumbing to its worldview.

I have approached this problem as a Christian, and since a substantial majority of our nation's citizens are professing Christians, the matter deserves their special attention. But the problem is by no means a "church" matter, for religion is no respecter of who attends or does not attend a particular service. The issue *is* a religious one, and I believe that this means it should be of interest and concern to everyone, since in everyone there burns—or at least smolders—that spark of interest in what is *really* real, what is of ultimate worth, and what we as individuals and as a people are today and what we can become tomorrow. Therefore, this book is addressed not only to "church people" but also to citizens—to human beings. The issue is not labels, but intent, not whether people are "religious," but whether they have religious concerns.

The structure of this book is straightforward. Chapter 1 describes what we already know about television and its power, and why religion is concerned about TV's cultural role. Chapter 2 enlarges the perspective to show that TV is actually an expression of the new technological era, and describes the church's inadequate response thus far to the challenges of the technological era.

Chapter 3 sets forth a Christian theological framework from which to analyze the world of television, and Chapter 4 then examines television—its myths, stories, values, and assumptions, in comparison with this Christian worldview. Chapters 5 and 6 describe in detail the best known of the church responses to the challenge of television—the electronic church—in both its positive and negative aspects. Chapter 7 suggests specific strategies for action in the mainline churches.

Chapters 8, 9, 10, and 11 consider the three ethical and public policy issues which must command our attention as we consider ways to respond to the challenges posed by television: violence and sexual violence; censorship and media regulation; and the global implications of our American media policies. For each issue I have proposed some "middle axioms" to give guidance for action and thus to bridge the gap that so often divides theory from practice.

Finally, Chapter 12 looks at some of the "signs of hope," specific ways individuals and groups can work in production and distribution, the influencing of public policy, and media education. The objective here is to help citizens avoid becoming either hopeless illiterates in this new media world, or unintentional religious heretics, but rather can respond with assurance and hope to the enormous potential of the world of television.

I want to acknowledge a number of people who had a part in making this book a reality. Les Brown of *Channels* magazine originally suggested I publish some of my essays which have found their way into these pages. Everett Parker, who got me involved in religious communication 30 years ago, has continued to provide insights, and he read and commented on several chapters. David Graybeal at Drew Seminary helped in conceptualizing the project. Coworkers at the Communication Commission of the National Council of Churches, D. Williams McClurken, David Pomeroy, and Herbert F. Lowe, read parts of the manuscript and made valued comments. Arie Brouwer, NCC General Secretary, provided the sabbatical leave time necessary for me to write the book. James M. Wall, editor of the *Christian Century*, read the manuscript and provided many helpful comments.

Others have made more indirect contributions through discussions over the past two decades. Annual meetings of the North America Section of the World Association for Christian Communication have provided a helpful forum for me to air a number of my ideas over the years. Members of the NCC Taskforce on Theology, Education and the Electronic Media, from 1984 to 1986, yielded many insights, as did presentations by George Gerbner, Gregor Goethals, Cees Hamelink, James Halloran, Herbert Schiller, and Robert White at a symposium on Religion and the Mass Media sponsored by Trinity Parish in 1983. The NCC Communication Commission's Special Study Commission on Violence and Sexual Violence in the Media, chaired by James Wall, provided a unique opportunity to study that complex issue during 1984–1986. Discussions over many years with Nelson Price of United Methodist Communications and Richard Heffner of the Motion Picture Association Classification and Rating Administration have been particularly illuminating, as were insights from the members of the National Coalition against Censorship, whose meetings I have been privileged to chair for the past decade. Stewart Hoover's research and George Conklin's communication models made valuable contributions.

Robert White and the Centre for the Study of Communication and Culture in London made available their unsurpassed communications library. European colleagues Manfred Linz, Hans Eckehard Bahr, Hans Wolfgang Hessler, Norbert Schneider, Neville Jayaweera, and the staff and members of the Central Committee of the World Association for Christian Communication, supplied helpful though sometimes disturbing perspectives on the American media scene.

Finally, it is difficult to overstate the contribution of my wife, Betty. She has read every word I have written, and her insights and thoughtful contributions are on every page. But more, she created the environment, encouragement and support without which this book would not have been possible.

One

THE WORLD OF TELEVISION

Wouldn't it be remarkable if, right before our eyes,
American television was trying to tell us as much
about ourselves as we can bear to know?

Richard Adler, *Television as a Cultural Force* (1976)

The Real World and the World of Television

For the first time in history, both children and adults are living in two
worlds. One is the reality system of face-to-face encounter with other
people, working at the office or store or home, taking care of the
children or visiting with neighbors, playing with the kids and tending
the yard, reading books and telling stories and remembering the past
and planning for the future.

We call this *the real world*.

The other is the far more vivid and appealing pseudoreality system
which provides instantaneous and transient sensation, immediate gratification, a flood of words and pictures in a never-ending, always-
available outpouring of moving images, but with no face-to-face relationships, no genuine experiences of learning from failures or suc-
cesses, no processing of data as when we read it, and almost no connection with our past or our cultural tradition.

We call this *the world of television*.

This book is about the new worldview of television, and its effect
on our culture. It is also about religion, which has a particular worldview of its own. And it is about the way religion and television are
today acting, interacting, and reacting over the question of who will
shape the faith and value system of our culture in the future, and what
the shape of that worldview will be.

What We Know about Television

We know a great deal about television, about who uses it, how it is used, and what effects it has on users. According to the A. C. Nielsen Company, in 1985 the television set was on in the average home seven hours and seven minutes a day. The average viewer watched about four hours and thirty minutes each day.[1] This amounts to 31.5 hours per week, or considerably more than one full day and night in every week of every month, year after year.

This single statistic means that, aside from eating, sleeping, and working, most people in America spend about 80% of their entire lives in the world of television rather than in the real world. Of course the television world does not completely exclude the real world, but families watch more than 45 hours each week, and in households with cable and subscription services the figure jumps to 58 hours, while most adults spend only 40 hours at work and children spend only 30 hours in school.[2]

Consider, for example, how an average family of four spends their seven hours "with TV" each weekday. By 4:30 in the afternoon Junior is home from school and has turned on the set to watch a robot cartoon from his usual sprawl on the floor. This is the beginning of almost continuous involvement with TV of at least some family members until they go to bed. They won't all be watching all the time. In fact, sometimes nobody will be watching. Often they will be doing something else while they are watching. But, like 86 million American homes each day, this family will become a part of the world of television.

Soon Dad comes home from work and watches some of the local 5:30 news while chatting with Sis. At dinner they view an old rerun of "All in the Family" or a game show and then finish with the evening news. For the next hour they will be in and out of the TV room (which used to be called "the living room"), leaving the set tuned to a game show such as "Wheel of Fortune" or "The Newlywed Game."

Just before eight o'clock they all gather to discuss whether to watch the "Bill Cosby Show" (Sis's favorite), "Magnum, Private Eye" (Junior's favorite), or an old movie which Mom and Dad saw years ago and would like to see again. As a compromise, they switch channels back and forth during the commercials, and, if Mom and Dad give up, may very possibly stay with the new music-TV channel which entrances both Junior and Sis, who at this point may be doing part of their homework at the same time.

The evening continues. Phone calls come and go. Mom sends Junior off to bed. Dad goes over to the desk and pays some bills. Sis, her homework spread out before her, watches part of the "Merv Griffin" show and "Night Court" before leaving to wash her hair. Dad picks up the evening news before turning the set off at 11:30.

According to the statistics, that's an average evening in an average American home. "Average" means that for every family watching four hours a day, another family is watching *ten* hours a day. It is important to note that America is the only nation in the world today whose citizens spend most of their leisure time in the world of television. For Europeans and Japanese, the average viewing is between one to three hours per day, and in the rest of the world it is far less. Americans spend between two to seven times more hours living in the world of television than any other people on earth.

And what effect is all this television viewing having on us? Again, research tells us a great deal about the effects. Returning to our typical family, if Junior is like 40% of his fellow fourth-graders, he is watching five hours or more of television daily. His time spent watching television is time *not* spent doing something else, such as developing motor skills through play, or social skills through being with other kids, or conceptual and creative skills through hobbies, or developing imagination and logical abilities through reading.

And if Sis is like her friends, she will have logged 16,000 hours of television by the time she graduates from high school—more time than she will have spent in classes from kindergarten through 12th grade. She will have watched something like 500,000 commercials. Her own tastes in clothes and music and her habits of behavior and speech may not have been directly shaped by television, if she has enough built-in skepticism and sales resistance. But the tastes and habits of her peers will have been influenced—otherwise the advertisers would not spend $19 billion a year on television ads—and *they*, in turn, will largely influence and shape her tastes, habits, and values.

Here are some of the other, more sobering findings about the effects of television on children.[3]

● Children who are heavy users of television (four hours or more a day) typically do worse in school than light viewers, although there is

some evidence that watching TV helps low IQ students in some subjects.

● Watching television depresses reading skills.

● Watching television does not encourage an expansion in language
skills.

● Watching television reinforces violent behavior.

● Children are strongly influenced by commercials. Below the age
of eight most children do not understand that commercials are designed
to sell something, yet they are the targets of sophisticated sales techniques.[4]

Television reinforces divisions between rich and poor, black and
white, male and female. Black students watch more TV than Hispanic
students, who, in turn, watch more than white students. Children of
parents with less education watch more, and, at the fourth-grade level,
boys watch more TV than girls. Heavy viewing is associated with poor
academic performance, which makes these findings particularly trou-
blesome.

On the other hand, television serves many socially useful purposes.
From the point of view of the advertisers, television is the keystone
of our economic system. Without television to teach people what to
buy, and, indeed, to teach them *to* buy, our vast production-consumption system would falter, perhaps even collapse. With more than
86 million homes using television sets (98% of all homes), our 1220
operating television stations, all but 113 of which are commercial,
reach more people more economically than does any other medium.
Recognizing its central commercial role, advertisers in 1984 spent $19
billion on television to get their message across to consumers.[5] This
was a very good bargain indeed, for it represented an outlay of a mere
$211 per household on the part of all the advertisers taken together,
in exchange for which they were able to reach virtually every person
in the nation, every day, all year long.

People like television. They find it entertaining, informative, and
interesting. They would like to spend their spare time with it almost
as much as with friends. More than half the families in America frequently watch TV together—more than any other activity except having
meals together. People believe TV is doing "a better job" in the community than the churches, police, newspapers, schools, or their local
government. They get most of their news and information from TV

and find it the most credible news source compared with all other media.[6]

Here are some specific ways people find TV useful in their lives.

First, television provides people with an opportunity for *relaxation and escape.* Many viewers watch simply to pass the time, to get away from pressures, to enjoy. Michael Real points out that individuals driven by the Calvinist work ethic and our cultural consumer-ethic require opportunities to *do nothing.* Television is perhaps most useful to many people by allowing them to laugh, to get angry, to feel emotions, or even to be bored without feeling a sense of responsibility or a pang of conscience. Television often is criticized for its banality, its failure to challenge. But it is precisely this quality that appeals most to many people: they feel the need to escape momentarily from the pressures of life. Historically, every society has discovered some means of temporary escape for its citizens, ranging from orgiastic dancing and dramatic rituals to alcohol and opium. In comparison to many alternatives, television offers escape that is inexpensive, immediate, and socially acceptable.

Second, and closely related, television provides many people with important *psychological compensation* for their sense of alienation or frustration born of loneliness, poverty, illness, joblessness, loss of loved ones, divorce, and similar problems. For these people television is always there, accessible, available, a moving and speaking image in "living" color, compensating for a loss of contact in another part of their lives. Perhaps this explains why there are more TV sets than bathtubs in America: many people apparently need companionship and psychological compensation even more than cleanliness.

Third, television provides a sense of *security and stability.* One of the strongest messages of television is that life is not totally chaotic, that there is somebody in charge. Richard S. Salant, president of CBS News for 16 years, says that the nightly newscast on TV offers proof to the viewer that "the world's still here and there's going to be another day."[7] From Dr. Kildare to Marcus Welby, M.D., from Matt Dillon to Kojak, from Edward R. Murrow to Walter Cronkite and Dan Rather—we are assured that doctors heal, that law officers keep the peace, that the news is understandable and not too threatening, in other words, that the world is a place of reasonable security and stability.

Fourth, television brings us *information,* in vast quantities. It pictures the world for us, from the marvels under the sea to explorations of another planet. It slows the cheetah and speeds the unfolding of an orchid. It peers into the heart of the cell and backward in time. It is almost literally our window on the world. This is perhaps its most obvious, though not its most important, utility.

Fifth, television helps us to *cope*. It tells us how we should behave in the presence of the rich and of the poor, what teenagers should wear, what words are acceptable in polite society. It shows us how to pick a lock and how to defend ourselves against a mugger. It helps us deal with stomach upsets and dirty toilet bowls. And through careful attention to stereotypes and formula situations, from its soap operas to its dramas, television provides us with scenarios which we can use in dealing with real situations in everyday life.

Sixth, television gives us a sense of *belonging*. When a president is shot or a Challenger mission ends in disaster, we suffer as a nation—together. When the Rose Bowl Parade or the Superbowl is on, we know we can discuss it with everyone tomorrow because we will all "be" there today. In addition to this sense of the whole nation being together, television gives us a sense of belonging to individuals. As "Marcus Welby, M.D.," Robert Young received thousands of letters a year requesting personal medical advice. The three anchors of the nightly news are greeted routinely as Dan, Tom, and Peter by complete strangers, and for more than a decade Walter Cronkite was considered "the most trusted individual in America." Since these individuals belong to us, we belong to them—and to each other.

Finally, television provides us with a rich *fantasy* world. In recent years a whole new genre of "situation fantasies" has developed, taking us routinely to a forbidden island or to a love boat—as if it were a perfectly normal thing to do. Music-TV has added a new level of vivid stream-of-consciousness visuals to rock music which excites the fantasy life of youth, just as "Love Boat" excites the fantasy life of their elders. And in both cases television is sufficiently removed from the real life of viewers so that the experience can be both exciting and safe.

Indeed, we do know a great deal about the effects of television, both the good and the bad. But these are merely the surface effects of television's deeper power. They do not explain the primary role of television at all.

The Hidden Role of Television

There is a hidden role of television which transcends all of these surface effects. The primary, but hidden, role of television is to tell what our world is like, how it works, and what it means. Dean George Gerbner at the Annenberg School of Communications in Philadelphia says that television acts as "the cultivator of our culture."[8]

While it is true that television is having a profound effect on us as it succeeds or fails at entertaining, informing, and selling, somehow we have to back off and try for a broader perspective. For behind the entertainment, the information and the selling, something far more important is going on.

Imagine that we are in a boat, rowing across a vast, slow-moving river so large that we cannot even see the other side. We view other boats moving back and forth. Some are faster than others, some larger and carry more wealth, some are going different directions. But all of us—ourselves and those we are observing—are unaware that *all of us are being moved by the river itself.* Similarly, as we move through the world of television, some programs are more effective, some more costly and entertaining, others go off in educational or special-interest directions. But all of them—and ourselves—are being changed from what we were to what we will become, by the *process of television itself.*

This developmental process, this slow change, takes place constantly as we watch the television images. The process goes on regardless of what program is viewed at a given moment. It is present in every sit-com, every soap opera, every movie, every newscast and commercial—regardless of whether the particular program is in good taste or bad, high art or kitsch, pandering or profound.

What is happening is that the whole medium reflects and expresses the myths by which we live. These myths tell us who we are, what we have done, what power we have, who has power and who does not, who can do what to whom with what effect, what is of value and what is not, what is right and what is not. It also tells us what has happened, and what has not. It takes our history and our present and interprets it to us. In a sense, television coverage of events is less concerned with history than with what the medium itself believes ought to be remembered. It thus becomes a kind of collective memory of our shared experiences. One need only think back to what we remember of major events—the deaths of presidents or the waging of war, for example—to realize that most of what we remember is in fact what the images television has fashioned on our behalf. The same is true of our present.

It is here that much of the research and discussion about television has proved to be fruitless, or even diversionary. By focusing on how TV sells a product, on who is "ahead" in the Nielsen ratings, on whether a particular program was canceled or censored or sponsored or not, we have missed the larger issue. By trying to get people excited about liberal bias in the news, or nudity or profanity in a particular program, or the ideological bent of a certain series, or whether a network is "Christian," we have diverted the attention of many concerned citizens from the most important problem, the basic point, namely, that *the whole process of television is providing us with a worldview which not only determines what we think, but also how we think and who we are.*

The research community itself must assume part of the blame for pointing our attention in the wrong direction. James Carey has shown that the past 30 years have been grounded in the "transmission" or "transportation" view of communication: who says what to whom with what effect. This is communication as business sees it, as the process of transmitting messages at a distance for the purpose of control.[9] By contrast, European researchers have seen communication much more as a process through which a shared culture is created, modified, and transformed. They have stressed the view that communication is not directed toward the extension of messages, but toward the maintenance of a society.

Primarily, however, it is the media industry itself that has been driven by attempts to develop theories and practices which would bring about certain predictable kinds of behavior—to get people to try a new life-style, to prefer one product over another, to vote for a particular candidate, and so on. Thus, to return to our river analogy, while both researchers and industry leaders have been able to map with considerable accuracy the directions and speeds of various boats carrying packets of "information" across the waters (e.g., in the Nielsen ratings or motivational research), they have failed to relate their maps to the movement of the river as a whole (the changes in the entire culture). And as a result, the public has never had the information it needs to give serious consideration to the overall impact of television.

Carey urges researchers in America to deal with communication more as a cultural study. This is what the general public must do as well. Cultural studies seek to understand human behavior and to interpret its significance, to look at TV, for example, and to diagnose its human meanings. Carey proposes that human behavior be considered as a text, with the task of the researcher being to construct a "reading" of the text. He likens this to the discipline of hermeneutics: "Our 'texts' are not always printed on pages or chiseled in stone—though sometimes they are. Usually, they are texts of public utterance or shaped behavior. But we are faced just like the literary critic with figuring out what the text says, of constructing a reading of it."[10]

In a modest sense, this is the approach followed in this book, as we examine "texts" in the world of television and construct a "reading" of them in order to surmise their meaning for society as a whole.

The Concern of Religion

But why should *religion* be concerned with the cultural role of television? Granted that there are many church-sponsored programs on television, and that church people want to get their messages across to the wider public, just as educators, artists, vegetarians, Rotarians, and many other concerned groups in society want to get their ideas expressed. What is unique about the interest of religion in television's role in society?

Here it is important to state what is meant by religion. While attendance at church services may be one index of religiosity, it certainly is not a sufficient one. Neither is adherence to a particular creed, nor membership in a particular church, nor support of "religion in general." I propose as a good working definition one suggested by Donald Miller: religion is that set of symbolic expressions and activities which (1) reflect a person's attempt to give ultimate meaning to life, and (2) justify one's behavior and way of life, conscious of the certitude of death and the pervasiveness of human suffering.[11]

If this is the way we define religion, then we can see that television and religion are on a kind of collision course in American culture today. It is not that television and religion are simply providing different ways of looking at the world. Science, art, and religion all represent different ways of describing the same experiences, and they need not be antagonistic. Nor is it that television has replaced religion's information-giving role, though it is true, as Tawney says, that in the Geneva of

Calvin's day, the pulpit was both lectern and press, while today the church's monopoly on information has been effectively usurped by the mass media. The challenge is much more fundamental: in many ways television is beginning to *replace* the institution that historically has performed the functions we have understood as religious. Television, rather than the churches, is becoming the place where people find a worldview which reflects what to them is of ultimate value, and which justifies their behavior and way of life. Television today, whether the viewers know it or not, and whether the television industry itself knows it or not, is competing not merely for our attention and dollars, but for our very souls.

It is not only our individual souls that are at stake, but also the soul of our nation. Robert Bellah's study of the roots of American democracy led him to conclude that during the nation's early life "the real school of republican virtue in America . . . was the church." The church was not only the first true institution in American society, but it "gave the first lessons in participation in the public life." Bellah cites Alexis de Tocqueville's observation that "it was the mores that contributed to the success of the American democracy, and the mores were rooted in religion." [12] In a sense it is these mores, these moral attitudes or what Tocqueville has called "the habits of the heart" which are at risk if the mass media in general, and television in particular, succeed in replacing the church as the place where the mores are generated and sustained.

Of course it is the whole culture, not just television, which supplies us with these mores and with our worldview of meaning. Without a culture we would simply cease to be human, and what our particular culture holds to be good, true, and beautiful are what we as humans by and large also find to be good, true, and beautiful. It was this reality that Emile Durkheim referred to when he wrote, not that religion is a social phenomenon, but that "society is a religious phenomenon." [13]

In many ways culture comes down to who you remember, what you remember, and when you remember. Television is rewiring the collective nervous system of our particular culture, and in doing so is beginning to determine the answers to all three questions. For while it is true that culture expresses itself through every form of communication: face-to-face, family, school, work, recreation, and so on, today television is assuming the dominant role of expression in our lives. Television is becoming the primary expression of the mores and the meanings—the real religion—for most of us.

This means that *television is itself becoming a kind of religion,* expressing the assumptions, values, and belief patterns of many people in our nation, and providing an alternate worldview to the old reality, and to the old religious view based on that reality, for millions of viewers. As we shall see, the values, assumptions, and worldview of television's "religion" are in almost every way diametrically opposed to the values, assumptions, and worldview of Christianity and the historic Judeo-Christian tradition in which the vast majority of Americans profess to believe.

Paul Tillich has said that "the substance of culture is religion and the form of religion is culture." [14] His concept has profound implications for the roles of both television and religion in our society. It means that television, which has become the prime cultivator of our culture, is providing us with the myths, teachings, and expressions of our religion, whether or not we recognize it. It also means that churches and religious schools and seminaries must take a new and completely different view of the profound role television is assuming in our culture, unless they are prepared to abdicate their own role as the place where people search and find meaning for their lives.

The question is not whether we face a religionless future. People are going to continue to ponder the fundamental meaning of life and to give it expression in ritual, myth, and celebration. The question is *where* the ultimate questions about the significance of life and one's moral responsibility are going to be asked, and from what source will come the proposed answers. Whether the churches will continue to play the role they have played historically in America depends on whether they can provide a better context for pondering, celebrating, and working out the meaning of people's lives than alternative sources can. And by far the most powerful alternative to the churches that is emerging as we approach the end of the 20th century is the world of television.

TWO

THE TECHNOLOGICAL ERA'S THREAT TO RELIGION

This world of ours is a new world, in which the unity
of knowledge, the nature of human communities, the
order of society, the order of ideas, the very notions
of society and culture have changed and will not return
to what they have been in the past.

Robert Oppenheimer (1963)

The Technological Era

While it is true to say that television is challenging the central role of
the church today, this is not nearly the whole truth. The religions of
the world are experiencing not merely competition from new and appealing media but also fundamental challenge from a new worldview.
We are facing not only a new age of information, but also a new
technological era which brings with it a challenge to all of the historical
religions, and which can lead either to humankind's next integrative
steps toward new religious insights and meaning, or to a collapse of
religious development and the emergence of a period of anarchy and
despair.

It is not enough to call what we are experiencing today "rapid social
change" or even "revolution," since these connote only social or political upheaval. The change is more basic in that it modifies everything
we have known before. The Dutch theologian Arend van Leewen suggests that there have been only two basic eras in all of history. The
first was the ontocratic era in which we have lived until now. From
the first written histories and for 5000 years thereafter, human society

always apprehended life as a cosmic totality, where belief in a God or gods outside human experience held together the contradictory and confusing elements of the human community. But relatively suddenly, within the last 300 years or so, we have moved away from this unifying concept into a multiform system of relationships, with no specific cornerstone, no single integrating element which gives all other things their reason for being. We have moved into the technological era, and this is the great new fact of our time.[1]

The technological era is functional and pragmatic, characterized by utilitarianism and relativism. It is supported by three philosophical views. The first is *rationality*, the idea that meaningful lives must be amenable to reason. The second is *autonomy*, which holds that people can find in themselves and their world the norms and goals for their own existence. The third is *humanism*, which asserts that this space-time world is the proper home for humankind, and rejects metaphysical claims ("they will be rewarded in heaven by and by") and demands that religion deal with the here-and-now.

Taken together, these three views describe secularization, which is not necessarily inconsistent with the Christian faith. Harvey Cox has pointed out that secularization is, in Dietrich Bonhoeffer's words, "man's coming of age," a freeing from the bondage of all closed metaphysical systems.[2] Unfortunately, this new-found freedom thus far has resulted in people being treated as means rather than as ends. The technological era has created a world of means, which replaces people as the center of meaning. Jacques Ellul calls this force we have created The Technique, by which he means a style of conduct that pervades our life and governs all of our personal and social activities—a kind of morality. The Technique is essentially a method of problem solving. It asks: How can we best solve this problem *now*? rather than: What is the ultimate objective and how can we reach it? The means is identified with the end, and whatever gets something "done" is good.[3]

Already the communication manifestations of The Technique resemble Aldous Huxley's *Brave New World* brought to life. The Technique's communication does not use fear or threats, nor does it concentrate on undermining its opponent. Rather it woos people, taking their own genuine needs (to be safe, to be liked, to be comfortable), and then using these needs to create other needs which make people not only willing but quite eager to agree with what is being said, to buy what is being sold (the deodorant, the beer, the antacid). A glaring example of the problem this creates is the present state of television news on the TV networks; most people *prefer* its simplistic presentation over a more complex and demanding one, and, by pandering to this preference, TV encourages the least, rather than the most, from individual viewers.

This new technological worldview and its communication manifestations are achieving a remarkable unity of acceptance everywhere—not only among the capitalist West and the communist nations, but even from the less technically developed nations. It has been given a tremendous boost by the development of the multinational corporations which treat the whole world as a stage in their competition for economic profits. By enabling new flows of money, information, and power on a world scale, the multinationals have succeeded in insulating themselves from both political and social constraints on their economic power, and thus have become an embodiment of the supreme value of economic efficiency over human values. It is only recently, as workers in America's Rustbelt, milltowns, and silicone valleys begin to see their jobs being shifted to workers in Southeast Asia, that the multinational's dehumanizing policies have come close enough to home to attract popular attention. But the problem is much more serious than the loss of American jobs, because in the new technological worldview, not just Americans but *everyone* is expendable.

The Technological Worldview's Challenge to Religion

The new technological worldview poses three specific threats to religion. First, it is diverting a major portion of the world's interests, motivations, satisfactions, and energies away from a religious center—*any* religious center. In Europe this is symbolized by the churches' having become empty shells, visited only as objects of architectural interest, and in the United States by the growing chasm between what churchgoers profess and how they act. Elsewhere in the world, religion functions primarily in its superstition modes (as in much of central Africa), or is used as a device for social or political control (as in Iran, India, and the Middle East).

Second, it is robbing genuine religious vocabularies of their power. The symbols, rites, images, and references of religion no longer move people. Today most people in the First World relate to—that is, understand, recognize, and think about—the images of "Dallas" and

"Dynasty" far more than they relate to the images of Abraham, Moses, and Paul. Biblical images, and most historical Christian images as well, no longer have the power to move, to motivate, to illuminate, to instruct. Rather, they have become relics—quaint oddities not to be taken seriously but only to be treated gingerly as part of a bygone culture.

Third, the new technological environment encourages the growth of religious concern which has little or no interest in organized religion. Creative and dynamic religious forces are finding expression not only in film, literature, and the arts, but also in some aspects of science and industry, where people are seeking ways to give institutional expression to their basic religious concerns while at the same time rejecting alliances with institutional religion. Alcoholics Anonymous, drug rehabilitation centers, coalitions for social and political reforms, therapy clusters, the adult education movement—these and other activities provide opportunities for people to "get involved," without the benefit of clergy. *Parachurch* activities are emerging in Western culture as a growing expression of religious faith which rejects the traditional organizational expressions of that faith.

While it is encouraging to see religious concerns permeate the secular culture, at the same time social reform without a vital connection to religious conviction tends to end in disillusionment and cynicism. On one hand, organized religion needs to find expression in practical social services and should encourage the development of these parachurch activities. On the other hand, such activities require the perspective of biblical faith which seeks the kingdom of God on earth without falling into the illusion that we are going to bring this kingdom into being by our own actions or that we can expect to participate in it within our own time. Without a connection to the religious community and the theological corrective it brings, parachurch activities tend to become either self-serving and cynical, or else shortsighted and naive in their expectations of bringing about permanent social reform in our time.

The New Media Environment

Each of these three threats to religion is manifested clearly and powerfully in the mass media. Television makes the secular alternatives to traditional religious values tremendously appealing. It has supplanted the traditional religious vocabulary with a new "religious" vocabulary comprised of a curious mix of economics, science, high technology, and fantasy. Examples of this new vocabulary are found in films such as George Lucas's "Star Wars," where Luke (sic) Skywalker and his pals fly high-tech versions of jet airplanes against Darth Vader, a literal prince of Darkness; in Stanley Kubric's "2001," where the computer HAL exemplifies the marriage of high-tech with human qualities, including the will-to-power; and Stephen Spielberg's "Close Encounters of the Third Kind" and "E.T.," where good guy extraterrestrials appear in majestic supertechnological millennialisms.

At the same time, persons and situations in the real world who possess genuine religious motivation and action become secularized by their presentation on TV. Television first glamorizes them by giving them celebrity status, and then robs them of their religious rootage by making them indistinguishable from secular media events and personalities. Even a Martin Luther King Jr. or a Mother Teresa have not been strong enough religious images completely to escape television's powerful and crushing ability to commercialize and secularize every person and event that come under its scrutiny.

Although we have lived within this new media environment for only a few decades, some of its characteristics are becoming clear:

● An increasing dependence on mediated communication as distinct from face-to-face communication; more time spent with electronics, less spent with people.

● An increasing number of communication delivery systems, together with a greater diversification of programming, so that individuals can pick and choose only those messages which reinforce *already held* attitudes and beliefs. This results in cultural fragmentation whereby people literally *cannot hear or see* others.

● A shift from treating communication as a service function essential to the welfare of the whole society (like water and roads) to treating it as a commodity to be purchased and sold. As media structures are increasingly controlled by the laws of economics, they inevitably become larger and more monopolistic, and at the same time less and less related to any system of morality.

● A trivialization of all news, information, and entertainment for the vast majority of people, with emphasis given to information rather than meaning, surface events rather than depth and reflection. At the same time, sophisticated communication facilities are available to a small elite for their personal growth, education, and enrichment, through computer programs, data bases, specialized videocassettes, and a wide assortment of information services. This encourages the growth of a new two-class society: the information-rich and the information-poor.

As the technological era permeates cultures worldwide, the mass media are increasingly employed as a tool of the production-consumption cycle rather than as a source of the education, information, and entertainment required for the well-being of all people, an element essential to the development of citizens in any democracy. First in the United States, but now more and more in Europe, Japan, and elsewhere, television is being used essentially for only one thing: to deliver an audience to an advertiser (or to a government).

Listeners and viewers increasingly are being treated as commodities rather than as persons. As this trend becomes more pronounced, the information which is necessary for citizens to make the kind of informed decisions which could reverse this trend is itself becoming increasingly scarce, so that eventually the mass media will be able to provide only circuses for the masses who embrace it gladly and no longer can tell what they are missing.

This scenario is not some nefarious scheme hatched by a handful of persons bent upon destroying the social fabric. Rather, the process is simply the inevitable working out of The Technique worldview, which is means-oriented toward solving problems rather than teleologically oriented toward goals and values. Nor is the process characterized by an iron fist media domination or a carefully scripted propaganda campaign along the lines of Hitler's "Triumph of the Will" at Nuremberg. Rather, the media merely provide a soothing and comfortable environment which makes very few demands and is thus gladly embraced by the listener-viewer.

Neil Postman contrasts this difference between media as police state and media as trivializer in terms of the very different predictions about future media control proposed by George Orwell and Aldous Huxley, respectively. Orwell's *1984* envisioned a future in which Big Brother would use the mass media to turn society into a vast prison, where television would both spy on each citizen's every move and also supply an unending barrage of false propaganda thoroughly to brainwash the hapless public. On the other hand, Huxley in *Brave New World* suggested that "in the age of advanced technology, spiritual devastation is more likely to come from an enemy with a smiling face than from one whose countenance exudes suspicion and hate. In the Huxleyan prophecy, Big Brother does not watch us, by his choice. We watch him, by ours."[4]

There could scarcely be a better description of our present situation than Huxley's *Brave New World.* We are dominated not by force but by trivialization, by infantile gratification, by what Kierkegaard called "twaddle." Trivialization is inevitable in the world of the technological era, with its emphasis upon utilitarian means rather than truthful ends. Says Postman: "There is no Newspeak here. Lies have not been defined as truth nor truth as lies. All that has happened is that the public has adjusted to incoherence and has been amused into indifference."[5]

Paul Tillich had a term for that which stands at the very opposite of Christian grace and love. He called it the demonic. The term is used here in a special way. It does not mean the embodiment of everything evil in the world, nor the objectification of the ungodly. Rather, the demonic is located in society wherever there is found a unique combination of *genuine creative power* together with *perversion* of Christian values. The demonic affirms that which is less than God and pretends it is God: money, power, prestige. It operates in the individual's willful yielding to the temptation to give rein to the libido of sensuality, of power, and of knowledge, and it operates even more powerfully in human institutions than in individuals.

The power and perversion of commercial television in the United States today can be said to be demonic in this special sense. Scarcely any better description could be given to television's unique cultural role than that provided by Tillich in 1948, long before television arrived on the scene.[6] For during the past 30 years commercial television has become a powerful embodiment of form-creating and value-destroying energy in our lives.

The Church's Inadequate Response

Religious leaders have been painfully aware of both the fundamental shift to the technological era and of the new information techniques which communicate its worldview, but their responses have been largely inadequate. They recognize that there has occurred a major shift in values and assumptions, and they have responded in ways that reflect the historical responses which religion has always given to the challenges of opposing worldviews.

After all, this situation is nothing new to the Christian church. Christians *always* have found themselves at odds with the dominant values and assumptions in secular society. Today the problem may be different in degree, if van Leewen is correct. But Christians have always had to face the problem of how to respond to the cultural situation which is always more or less antithetical to their faith.

H. Richard Niebuhr suggested that there are five typical relationships of the Christian and society, seen both in history and in contemporary life:[7]

1. *Christ against culture* is the approach that requires Christians to abandon wholly the customs and institutions of the "heathen" society and to withdraw, either physically or by rejecting society's norms. Puritans of every age have taken this course, following the injunction, "Do not love the world or the things in the world" (1 John 2:15). This pattern is seen in monastic orders and various sects.

2. *Christ of culture* suggests that there is fundamental agreement between the values of church and society. Jesus is the great hero/teacher who, in concert with democratic principles, works to create a peaceful, cooperative society. This is seen in cultural Protestantism, and wherever the church reflects the values of culture.

3. *Christ above culture:* Christianity brings the culture up to a higher level of fulfillment; culture leads people to Christ, but Christ then enters into the situation from above with gifts which human aspiration cannot attain and "draws up" the society to higher levels of social attainment.

4. *Christ and culture in paradox:* this approach recognizes the necessity and authority of both Christ and culture, but also recognizes their opposition. Thus life is lived in faith precariously, sinfully, in tension between the demands of Christ and culture, in the hope of justification which lies beyond history. From Christ we receive the knowledge and freedom to do what culture teaches or requires us to do. This is exemplified by Martin Luther.

5. *Christ the transformer of culture:* human nature is fallen or perverted, and this perversion is transmitted by the culture; therefore Christ stands in judgment of all human institutions. But Christ also converts persons within their culture, through their faith and by turning away from sin and pride. Augustine, Calvin, and Wesley are examples.

Today the responses of various religious groups to the challenge of The Technique's communication have differed in ways that can be

illuminated by Niebuhr's model. For example, many biblical fundamentalists tend to reject the appeals of the mass media, and to a certain
degree to reject the media themselves. They sense the anti-Christian
value system it carries and counsel believers to return to religious
fundamentals which often include proscriptions against dancing, movies, plays, and rock concerts, and attempts at censorship of media,
especially films, TV, and books. At the same time they encourage
participation in church social events as a substitute for secular cultural
offerings. In some instances watching TV is prohibited, and in others
the faithful are encouraged to watch only "Christian" networks and
programs. Their "Christ against culture" position recognizes the seriousness of The Technique's appeal and its ability to lure people,
especially young people, away from fundamentalism's Puritan values.

The problem with the "Christ against culture" position is twofold:
first, strong reaction tends to increase the attractiveness of that which
is banished; and, second, the rejection of many cultural experiences
tends to leave persons psychologically involuted, intellectually isolat-
ed, and spiritually subject to the pride and authoritarianism generated
by any dogmatic and closed system.

Other so-called fundamentalists have taken just the opposite course,
that of the "Christ of culture." Having no doubt among themselves
about the answers to every religious question, they are led to the conclusion that the most important communication task is to reach others
with these answers and to convince them of their validity. They see
the success of The Technique in converting people to its value system,
and so they adopt these techniques—especially television, radio, and
books—to convert people to their own religious views. The "Christ
of culture" response characterizes most of the electronic-church
preachers, who, in the guise of rejecting the values of secular culture,
actually embrace them.

The "Christ of culture" view of many fundamentalists explains why
this segment of Christianity has been so quick to grasp every new
communication technique as it came along—first radio, then shortwave, motion pictures, television, and, more recently, cable, satellite
TV, and videocassettes. Theirs is the "pipeline" theory of communication: when the Christian message is reduced to a set of unvarying
verbal formulas, the only question is how to build a bigger and better
"pipe" through which to deliver the message to the recipient.

But while the programs of the "Christ of culture" advocates are rich in the vocabulary of 19th-century Christian evangelism, the images—and hence the real messages—resonate with The Technique, the gambits of modern television advertising. But using the techniques of commercial television and radio to achieve the end of Christian communication is self-defeating. The people who tune in the electronic evangelists are the already converted and convinced, and the programs they tune to are simply the techniques of the secular world used to reinforce views already held by those who are comfortable with an otherworldly, prescientific, anthropomorphic God superimposed on the underlying values of the technological era.

There is yet another "Christ of culture" response evident in religious mass media. These are the programs which appeal to many members of the mainline churches, people who go to church almost every Sunday, yet give little evidence of being uneasy about their deep involvement in secular culture and values. Robert Bellah has shown that most Americans today express a vague religious belief in God, but are utterly incapable of relating their faith to any kind of morally coherent life. "Feeling good" for them has replaced "being good," and relationships are based not so much on a religious conviction about the essential worth of every individual as they are based on contractual arrangements in which each person is considered of value to the extent that he or she is of value to *me*. The question, "Is this right or wrong?" is replaced by, "Is it going to work for me, now?"[8] What Bellah describes is one more manifestation of the value system of the technological era. By succumbing to this view while continuing to hold on to the trappings of mainline Christianity, many people in the mainline churches have adopted a "Christ of culture" response.

Both secular media and most religious media encourage these forms of cultural religion. In fact, its expressions, which are oblivious to the usual fundamentalist/liberal divisions, are perhaps the most pervasive of all religious responses. To be sure, these nominal Christians may find excesses in the media which are too gross even for thoroughly acculturated Christians to ignore—too much sex and violence in films, too many commercials on television, too much acid rain, too many armaments—but these are seen as problems which can be adjusted, reduced, and reworked, rather than as expressions of a fundamental clash with the center of their faith. For these "Christ of culture" Christians, the underlying values of commercial television are in fact *their* values.

An Alternative Response

There is a third response of Christians to the challenge of The Technique, a response which rejects both the "Christ against culture" and the "Christ of culture" views. It is hesitant, problematic, and ambiguous, but it tries to relate the requirements of historical Christian faith to the current cultural and media reality. It takes seriously the demonic power within the media but refuses to abandon them altogether. This alternative response is found to some extent in various mainline denominational and interdenominational groups in the United States, and in some of the established churches in Western Europe.

These church groups relate to the media at two levels. First, they produce programs in the media which, in the midst of the secular worldview and its power, try to illumine the human condition, to ask meaningful religious questions, to rediscover religious truths, and to make a beginning toward creating a new religious vocabulary which can have meaning and power for the multitudes. Such a response can have very little success in "worldly" terms, that is, in relation to audience size, income for stations and networks, or the development of national celebrities and media events which can be merchandized—criteria which normally signify success in the commercial media environment.

Second, these groups also work within the media industries themselves, and with the political institutions in the society, to bring about conditions which will allow the media to achieve their considerable potential for good. The objective here is to humanize the structures which govern the media, both by encouraging persons within the industry to "do well by doing good," and by insisting that the social and economic powers of the industry must be counterbalanced by governmental power which politically expresses the concern of citizens for the general public welfare. As in the case with program production, this media-reform approach is not likely to achieve significant success in "worldly" terms, since the power of The Technique and its media manifestations are so powerful, but, from a religious standpoint, the objective is nevertheless essential.

This dual approach tends to fit into Niebuhr's categories of "Christ and culture in paradox" and "Christ transforming culture." It recognizes the ambiguities and paradoxical nature of the church at work within a system full of powers which potentially corrupt everything they touch, including the church. At the same time it acts in the belief that testifying to the good news is a requirement which cannot be avoided, and that—potentially—faith and action based on this liberating gospel do indeed transform structures built upon human sin and pride.

This alternative approach rejects the utilitarian relativism characteristic of our ethos, and reasserts the radical monotheism of Christian history. It requires looking through and beyond the tempting simplicity of the technological era as communicated by television and the rest of the mass media. When confronted with a worldview so powerful, so seductive, and so effective in its ability to obscure and trivialize, what is required is a calculated and informed process of *unmasking* its messages. This unmasking, or demythologizing, of our television "text" requires of us the will to resist what is television's most powerful ally— our own inertia and tendency to let the images simply flow over us. It requires the discipline to deal with TV's images critically. It requires of the church that it supply the critical tools and context for the unmasking, which means that the images of television must become part of the sermonic and teaching elements of the church environment.

A major element in this unmasking of television's pretensions is the development of a sound theological basis for criticism. It is to this theology of communication that we turn next.

THREE

A THEOLOGY OF COMMUNICATION

The substance of culture is religion, and the form of religion is culture.

Paul Tillich, *The Interpretation of History* (1936)

What Is Theology?

Theology is a statement that tries to make sense out of our lives. Of course, there are more sophisticated views of theology. And there are many different kinds of theology—historical, systematic, practical, black, liberation—in fact, a "theology of" just about every movement and topic that requires serious thought and signification.

All of these theologies have at least one thing in common: they are attempts to deal honestly and lucidly with the way things are, so as to help people understand what life is all about.

Unfortunately, theology has become so specialized during the last 50 years that it has almost defined itself out of existence. Where only a few centuries ago theology was thought of as "the queen of the sciences," the one discipline that held all the others together and which everyone took with the utmost seriousness, today it speaks only rarely to the totality of the scientific world, and is almost nonexistent on the horizon of the average layperson. The theologians themselves seem to be disappearing. Not only are the massive systems of a Thomas Aquinas no longer produced, but for more than three decades we have not seen a single genuine systematic theology of the caliber of Gustav Aulén, Karl Barth, or Paul Tillich.

Avery Dulles charges that 20th-century theology has been largely a reaction against the corrosive influences of print culture on the faith of the church. Barthian neoorthodoxy sought to escape from the detached impersonality of the print medium by a revival of face-to-face oral communication as it existed in New Testament times. But the movement was fundamentally reactionary. It sought vainly to operate within a communications system—primitive oralism—that no longer existed. Dulles is right in insisting that the church "cannot wall itself up in a cultural ghetto at a time when humanity as a whole is passing into the electronic age."[1]

This chapter on a theology of communication is not an attempt to provide in any sense a genuine systematic theology. It is intended to provide a viewpoint from which to understand the workings of communication. It attempts to say what communication "is all about," in the context of what the world "is all about." It rejects some worldviews, and with them certain ways of using and thinking about communication. It proposes a worldview—a theological perspective—which I believe to be consistent with genuine biblical and historical Christianity, and which, if accepted by the reader, leads to certain implications about ways of using and thinking about communication.

What Is Communication?

The dictionary tells us that communication is: first, the act of transmitting; second, facts or information transmitted; third, written information, conversation, or talk; fourth, access between persons or places; or fifth, interchange of thoughts or opinions.[2]

The problem with all of these definitions is that they place communication in a third-party role, as if it were something that occurs *between* two people or things. None gives sufficient emphasis to communication as a *relationship* which involves persons and things, a relationship of which we are all an integral part. Trying to understand communication without these relationships is like trying to understand a human being through an autopsy: the life is missing.

I find more useful the following definition: *communication is the process in which relationships are established, maintained, modified, or terminated through the increase or reduction of meaning.* This allows us to examine the process of communication in a way which includes the "relateds" and how they are always affected as objects which become subjects, affecting and being affected, as well as the changes in meaning and in messages which become filled or voided of meaning as the process, and those related to it, constantly change.

Another problem with understanding communication is that it is so integral to what we mean by "human," and even to what we mean by "existence," that it is easy to use the term universally to include almost everything, and so to render the term quite meaningless. Arguments have been put forward that communication is education,[3] that it is the church,[4] that it is incarnation,[5] that it is Christianity.[6] While each of these conceptions contains helpful insights, and while in a sense communication is a constituent of everything, sometimes a more arbitrary and limited definition must be employed if the word is to be of practical value.

We need to explore both aspects of communication—its role as a part of everything, of all of being, and also how it functions in everyday life. The challenge at this point is a little like trying to understand water. Water is essential to all living things, and we need to understand that. But we also need a theory of hydrodynamics, which tells us how water *works*. We need both.

Therefore, we shall examine, first, how communication is essential to *being* (its ontological aspects); second, how communication functions in *society* (its ethical aspects); and finally, how communication *works* among practicing Christians today (its confessional, pastoral aspects).

Communication and Being

Most theologians today have abandoned serious attempts to develop arguments for the existence of God. Instead, they take an existential starting point, agreeing with Kierkegaard that existence precedes essence, that human beings decide in the act of existing. We no longer begin with a theory of reality or a theory of God, but can only begin where we are as human beings in the midst of all the contingencies of human experience.

What we discover is that, reduced to the most basic level possible, there exist only three things: matter, energy, and *relationships*. And these relationships, whether between atoms and molecules, bees and flowers, or humans and God, are created, sustained, and modified by some kind of communication. Another way of saying this is that everything relates to something, or else it does not exist, and within all relationships communication is present.

There is nothing outside our experience. Even that which we call the transcendent is understood as "that which exists in its own right beyond our categories of thought and explanation, but not necessarily that which is entirely outside our experience in all its modes."[7] One implication of this emphasis upon experience is that the deductive, the hypothetical, and the projective kinds of thinking no longer are controlling, but are replaced by the inductive, the coordinative, the analogical, and the dialogical.

It is significant that there is an increasing correspondence between recent Christian process theology and recent theories of communication. Process theology holds that things that endure are composed of a series or a process of distinct occasions or experience, each one connected to the next, and each one affecting the next. Nothing is independent and disconnected. All experience is related to previous experiences. Everything—atoms, animals, human beings, nature, and the universe—is interrelated. And *communication* is the fundamental process by which these relationships occur. Communication is a fundamental given of existence, essential to the nature of being.

In process theology the past is the totality of that which influences the present, and the future is the totality of that which will be influenced by the present. Each present moment is but a selective incarnation of the whole past universe. Our individual choices and actions, conditioned by the past, will make a difference throughout the future. And the mechanism that connects the past, present, and future is communication. We create our future by communicating our decisions. Since successful communication depends on the reduction of uncertainty, our communication options must be free to create new and wholly unprecedented relationships. This is what is meant by creating order out of chaos.

Community is where our human existence takes place. Community is established and maintained by the relationships created by our communications. We establish our relative individuality within this community. The more we participate in community, the more we become true individuals, and the more we become individuals, the more richly we participate in community.[8] Community, the fulfillment of effective human communication, is essential to our becoming human.

Language is necessary to human beings in community. Language shapes images and hence affects our actual sensibility and our modes of perception. Alfred North Whitehead wrote that "the mentality of mankind and the language of mankind created each other."[9] Walter Ong takes this a step further by holding that language and the media created by communication technologies are not simply instruments external to humans, to be used by them, but are in fact extensions and transformers of human beings.[10]

A similar view is taken by communication theoretician Harold Innis, who argues that communication technologies fashion media which bias individual perceptions of reality, and that different forms of communication technologies create different forms of social organization over knowledge.[11] Innis, Marshall McLuhan, and Edmund Carpenter all suggest that different media of communication bring about major shifts in human culture, along the following lines:

(1) Media are extensions of the human sensory apparatus.

(2) Media alter the internal sensory balance between eye, ear, and other organs.

(3) The dominant forms of media influence aesthetic preferences and all forms of social, political, and economic structure.[12]

The *freedom* which is essential in both communication theory and Christian theology is ideally suited for this cultural period in which ideological pluralism challenges the older forms of Christian dogmatics, and a radical reinterpretation of the biblical texts and the Christian tradition are necessary in order to do justice to recent scholarship. God is not absolute, omnipotent, wholly other; God is responsive. God's love is not controlling; it is persuasive. Christ is the force of creative transformation of the world, but this transformation depends for its actuality on the decisions of individuals communicating in their freedom.

The concept of the *interconnectedness of all things* makes possible a clearer understanding of the importance of ecological sensitivity in both the natural world and in economic theory where there is a systematic discounting of the future in order to justify overconsumption in the present. A corresponding interconnectedness appears in communication theory, which has moved away from the mechanical model of information/transmitter/ signal/receiver/audience (Shannon-Weaver, 1948), to models which at first added secondary relationships such as groups, neighborhoods, and social structures (Riley in 1958), then internal relationships such as self-images, abilities, media selection and so on (Gerhard Maletzke; Hamburg, 1963), until today the whole ecological system is recognized as part of the complex mix of communication experience. Communication models now embrace a never-ending, all-inclusive process, extending backward in time to take into account our personal and corporate history, and forward in time to take into account the future, involving other selves, families, communities, societies, and, ultimately, the whole of creation.[13]

In summary, communication in its most universal terms must be understood as a basic constituent of the process of being. But we also need to examine from a Christian perspective the role communication plays as *a process* which is used and misused in our experience as social and political beings.

A Christian View of Communication

As communication is central to maintaining any culture, so mass communication is essential to maintaining our highly technological culture. Mass communication is integral to mass production and mass consumption. It is the enabler of social communication. It acts as the nervous system of the social and political body, bringing together the sensations, responses, orders, sanctions, and repressions which are necessary for large accumulations of people to live together in community.

The mass media are not mere message carriers. They also confer power, legitimate systems, and provide ways of looking at the world. They supply the context in which information is learned, attitudes are formed, and decisions are made.

Christians living in our culture find themselves at odds with the assumptions and values within it. But the mass media echo these assumptions and values. Radio, television, newspapers, magazines, and the rest of the media seek out and detect those values and assumptions which appear to be acceptable in the culture. This is done without regard for any moral or religious considerations, since the media are a part of The Technique which is interested only in *what works*. The media then reproject these "valueless" values and assumptions back to its citizens, amplifying them in the process. Responses in the form of purchases, ratings, audience research, and so on, are then returned, indicating acceptance or rejection, and the media once again send back and amplify those values and assumptions which are found to have especially strong acceptance.

The process is one of *resonance*. Just as an organ pipe or a plucked string will vibrate to a particular frequency and amplify it naturally, so the mass media respond to those values and assumptions which find ready acceptance among the members of a particular culture and then amplify them. The question of whether television creates values and attitudes, or merely reflects them, is strictly a diversion, since the media, of course, do both. They reflect the values in the culture, and they legitimate, circulate, and amplify them and thus, in reality, "create" them as potent values, through the process of resonance. By choosing to repeat and amplify some of the myriad of possible values, attitudes, and worldviews, and not to repeat or amplify others, the media become a powerful process that helps to create, maintain, and change our culture, and those who become expert at finding and amplifying these messages feel no moral responsibility for *what* is resonated, but only that it is done well.

Thus a non-Christian view of life predominates in mass media, as it does in the society as a whole. As Martin Marty has pointed out, the "proper" opinion always dominates, and the Christian view is always the "improper" opinion.[14] Christians have a responsibility to speak out and act in response to their convictions and in opposition to views they believe to be false. But since we live in a pluralistic society, Christians must neither demand nor even expect that their own view must prevail, but rather insist only that it be heard and taken seriously, in faith that it will find adherents as, with varying degrees of success, it has throughout the past two millenia. The call is to be faithful, not triumphalist.

There are several Christian doctrines, derived from the witness of Scripture, Christian tradition, and the reflection of Christians today, which bear directly on the role of communication in society. They are: creation and stewardship; sin and redemption; the newness of life; good news and proclamation; and Christian witness.

1. That God is creator of "all things visible and invisible" is a central Christian doctrine. By this is meant that all things are interrelated, that the eternal order of things is revealed in the historical order, and that we human beings are not the creators but rather are bound together as part of creation along with all other parts of creation, in mutuality. Creation includes the techniques of social communication—the telephone, radio, television, movies, print, and so on. Without these technologies, humankind simply would be unable to live in the complex social structures we now enjoy.

Since all elements of social communication are first of all a creation of God, they must be thought of as being held in trust by those who use them. Stewardship is a necessary corollary of creation. The mass media are especially powerful forces in the society, and the importance of exercising stewardship in the use of them for good increases with the magnitude of their power.

The biblical record and Christian tradition are clear that human beings are expected by their Creator to use the good things of the earth to accomplish God's will: the building of a just, peaceful, and loving community. The media of social communication have enormous potential for aiding in this goal, and to use these techniques purely for self-aggrandizement and profit is completely ruled out by the Christian understanding of creation and stewardship.

2. Christians understand sin as the misuse of God's gifts. Sin is taking something that is a gift of God—things, money, power, prestige—and treating it as if it *were* God. Sin is not something that people are thrust into by events but is the result of choice, a choice not to live up to God's expectations for the full potential of all human beings, but rather to further the self at the expense of others. Humans constantly misuse the power over creation that God has given them. Instead of using their unique gifts to bring about harmony in all creation and its interrelatedness, they misuse power for selfish purposes.

The communication media have become a major source of power in the technological era. Because men and women depend upon them for information about their world, the media have become keys to many other forms of power: economic, social, and political. And precisely because of their intense concentration of power, they inevitably become a primary locus of sin. The primary manifestation of sin in the mass media is their treating persons as objects of manipulation and turning them into consumers of media rather than into participants through media.

Historically, Christianity has understood that a major role of government is the regulation of the misuse of power. A fundamental task of government is to protect the weak and defenseless against the powerful and the predator. It is only through the power of the whole state, acting on behalf of its citizens, by establishing limits to untrammeled exercise of power by the strong at the expense of the weak, that society can remain civil and community can remain intact. Thus Christians recognize the necessity for governmental regulation of those aspects of communication which allow it to become a monopoly of the few at the expense of the many.

3. Christian doctrine takes seriously the concept that God makes all things new, that novelty and creativity are essential elements of God's world. Therefore, Christians resist any attempts to restrict communication so that persons are restricted in their choices. New ideas, new values, new understandings are essential to growth and to human potential. Any policy or regulation which would restrict opportunities for persons to discover new meanings is theologically unsupportable.

Censorship of communication is itself a sin, since it allows one person or group to dominate the information intake of all others. Christian belief insists on remaining open to newness, and rejects attempts to restrain the way newness comes into the world. It also rejects top-down, one-way flows of communication. It remains open, not only to novelty, but also to that which is not yet completely understood, since God works in mysterious ways, and God's ways can never be fully grasped.

4. Christians testify to the fact of the good news that Christ came to set us free, that is, to set persons free from personal sin, from corporate bondage, and from all kinds of oppression—spiritual, mental, social, physical, economic, political. The good news is for every person, regardless of location or station in life. But since the good news is news of liberation, it has a definite bias toward those who are most in need of liberation—the poor, the weak, the defenseless. For Christians, a primary role of communication therefore is to aid in the process of liberation. The good news requires that communication in the community take into account all persons, and the whole person, and that it deal with them as sons and daughters of God. Communication that does otherwise, that treats persons as objects, is in fact oppressing them. Christians therefore have an advocacy role, to proclaim the good news and to work toward the fulfillment of its promise in the media of our times.

5. Finally, Christian doctrine challenges falsehood. Christianity is not evenhanded. It has a bias toward what it perceives to be real and true. The fact that we live in a pluralistic society means that as Christians we must be a witness for the truth as we perceive it while at the same time being open to hear the truth as perceived by others.

The social media communicate not only "messages." They also

establish a *way* of looking at everything. In this sense, they set the agenda as to what in society will be discussed and what will be ignored. Therefore, it is incumbent on Christians to challenge the media's view of the world if they believe it to be false. On the other hand, Christians support the political concept of pluralism, because it is an environment in which all persons may be heard. They have a responsibility to bring to bear their own vision and to attempt to influence the worldview of the media, while at the same time rejecting any temptation politically to enforce their views upon others.

The Nature and Content of Christian Communication

Communication in daily life is far less a cosmic process than that described at the beginning of this chapter, and is much more personal than the view of social communication just discussed. What we are dealing with here are the interactions between ordinary Christian people in everyday life. It involves such things as testimony, witness, evangelism, and telling the way one perceives the world, faith, and God.

In this context, *communication is the sharing of something experienced, by means of commonly understood relationships.* Reduced to its minimum, this kind of communication can be pictured as a process involving source-encoding-signal-decoding-destination. But in actuality, personal communication is a never-ending process which connects the "I" to other persons in continually developing feedback loops within a complicated field of relationships within culture, space, and time.

Each new generation has the task of taking the new technology of its age and rediscovering religious truths and making them meaningful in the light of cultural changes. This has always been a religious task. Each new cultural situation, shaped by the communication media of its time, reformulates the question, What does it mean to be human?

The answer to this question is being radically changed by the new media of communication. For example, we tend to think of two basic modes of communication, face-to-face and mass media. But between these two poles lie whole new combinations of communications processes which require us to redefine what is community and, therefore, what is human. By way of illustration: if I spend 30 minutes every day "with" my TV network newscaster, and I spend no time at all with the apartment dweller who lives next door, who then is my neighbor?

What does it mean to be "with"? What does "neighbor" mean? And if several people watch a TV evangelist each day and regularly discuss their experiences together, is this the church? What is "church"? What is "community"?

The following are some middle axioms for consideration. They are not basic theological principles, nor are they specific proposals for action, but rather come between principle and practice—they are middle axioms. The purpose is to state the axioms and then consider their implications for Christian living. These middle axioms are clustered around four aspects of Christian life: Christianity as communication; revelation as communication; the church as communication; and distortions of communication.

Christianity as Communication

Christianity can be understood as a religion of communication. Johannes Heinrichs[15] and Avery Dulles,[16] among others, have pointed this out. One reason that the Christian trinitarian view of God is important is that for the first time in history a dialogical—that is, communicational—view of the deity was put forward; God is both before us, with us, and in us. The doctrine of the incarnation represents God's self-giving, communicative action toward creation. The doctrine of redemption takes place through a communication process which allows us to maintain and to increase our sense of identity, an awareness of who we are, by means of interacting with and contributing to the total society. And love, the essential Christian message, can be made manifest only by "credible preaching by word and deed, on the one side, and by practical commitment (i.e., faith) on the part of the recipient."[17]

Religious communication between human beings may be "anonymously Christian," that is, it may occur even when the name of Jesus Christ is not mentioned, since communication about what is ultimately real is not exclusively Christian. Nevertheless, the entire content of Christian faith is "nothing other than the development of the dialogical principle itself," and "the relationship to God is not simply communication. It is rather that which makes communication possible."[18]

If we take Heinrichs's analysis as a starting point and at the same time accept the requirement that theology must at all times take into account the meanings present in common human experience, then *for Christians the aim of communication is to help people interpret their existence in the light of what God has done for them as manifest in Jesus Christ.*

This means that the purpose of Christian communication is *not* to ask, "How can we communicate the gospel in such a way that others will accept it?" This is the *wrong* question, the public relations question, the manipulative question, the question asked by the electronic church. Rather, our task is to put the gospel before people in such a way that it is so clear to them that they can accept it, or reject it—*but always for the right reasons.* As Tillich points out, it is better that people reject the gospel for the *right* reasons than that they accept it for the *wrong* reasons.[19]

Of course, one can never know with certainty what are the exactly "right" and "wrong" reasons for someone else, any more than we can know perfectly the innermost thought of others. Therefore, in fashioning our strategy of communication about the faith we can only act in faith, never in certainty. But our objective should always be to present the gospel in ways so clear and self-evident that the recipient will have an "Aha!" experience, so that the good news will make complete sense to his or her own inner world, so that the recipient will say, in effect, "I already knew that!"

Revelation as Communication

How is the Christian faith authentically communicated? How does revelation, or knowing about God, take place? H. Richard Niebuhr helpfully distinguishes between two ways in which we know: our external history and our internal history.[20]

External history is that set of experiences which are available to everyone: they are events, ideas, actions, experiments that can be duplicated. External events are impersonal. In the Christian tradition, they include such things as the "historical Jesus" and the Dead Sea Scrolls.

Internal history is a personal story about "our" time. Although it, too, deals with events that are verifiable by the community, it is not objective in the sense of a physics experiment or hieroglyphics written on the wall of an Egyptian tomb. The time involved is *our* duration. The history is *our* history. The experience is present in *our* memory. In the Christian tradition, this would include such things as our knowledge of Martin Luther King Jr. or Archbishop Tutu, or our experience with a sanctuary church or a peace march.

The task of Christian communication is to reveal our internal history, and the internal history of our community, in such a way that it will help individuals ask what meaning life holds for *them* and their community and internal memory. The content of Christian communication is not a series of logical propositions, or wall charts with connected squares "explaining" God's plan, or texts from the Bible committed to memory, or creed, or theological statements. The content of Christian communication is essentially what God has done in the lives of individuals, including me. There are many points of potential contact—history, nature, group experiences, individual's stories, the Bible. The content may be logical or charted or related to biblical passages or theologies—or it may not. What is important is that the content explains the internal history of the communicator and results in the recipient gaining perspective on the nature of what is ultimate reality, that is, the way things really are.

In terms of communication, it is important to note that it is not the words or content or things in themselves which are revelatory, but the *relationships of meaning* which are communicated. This means that authentic Christian communication is possible, not only in face-to-face relationships, but also in much more remote relationships, including those provided in and through the mass media—provided that relationships of meaning are communicated.

On the other hand, communication theory and sheer common sense tell us that the difficulty of successful communication increases with the *relational distance* one perceives. (Note that real physical distance is not what is important, but rather *perceived* relational distance. One can "be" very close to one's wife during a 3000 mile telephone conversation, or "be" very distant from the president who passes only 20 feet away in a swiftly moving motorcade.) Great relational distance makes Christian witness via the mass media difficult, complicated, and problematic. The same holds true for any communication that is remote in space or time: the greater the perceived distance between those communicating, the more difficult the communication of meaning becomes. This is true simply because the authentic source ("*my* story") is less available, less present, less accessible to the perceiver.

For example, the personality appearing on TV is not "really" present; the taped program is not in "real" time; and I cannot affect a televised program I am watching in any real way. It is this combination of remoteness of mass media technology *and* remoteness of space and time that makes Christian communication via television difficult, though not altogether impossible.

However, the mass media are technically ideal for the task of helping *prepare* people to hear and to receive the gospel. Mass media can provide education about the faith and stories about people and communities acting out of their religious convictions. It can examine issues and illuminate subjects which can help individuals understand themselves better, to bring them closer to reality, and to encourage them to ask the right questions about the meaning of life and the meaning of *their* lives, as well as to learn what Christians say and how they act regarding their involvement with the gospel.

To be revelatory, communication must take place within community. Communication cannot be validated unless it is affirmed in and through the life of persons in community. For this reason, the disintegration and rearrangements of community in America today pose a major challenge to effective Christian communication. Bellah, in *Habits of the Heart,* has documented this fragmentation of community.[21] He points out that in colonial times individual independence and social cooperation went hand in hand, but that this tradition grew out of two incompatible models of the relationship of the individual to society. The covenant model promised care and concern for others in exchange for divine care and concern. The contract model joined people together only to maximize their self-interest. During the past two centuries, individual fulfillment has gradually eroded the sense of community until today the *individual* tends to be the reference point for all values. This kind of secular freedom undermines human commitment since it treats *everything* as a dispensable commodity—marriage, friends, jobs, churches, religions, God—since everything has value only insofar as it has utility for the individual.

This analysis underscores the urgency of redefining and rebuilding community. From a Christian's point of view, it is only through the resurgence of community that the individual can reconnect with God who is manifest in the process of participation and whose essence is relatedness, wholeness, and harmony. Given the new technological era with its rapid growth of the means of mass communication, new forms of community will have to be invented, identified, and constructed which take these media into account. Only as we succeed in maintaining and recreating community will we be able to meet the needs of the new humanity.

The Church as Communication

All of creation is potentially a mediator of divine disclosure, but the church is the community which possesses the greatest potential for communication about God. According to Avery Dulles, "The Church exists in order to bring men into communion with God and thereby to open them up to communication with each other.[22] This task is variously called "mission," "evangelism," or "education."

Since the apprehension of God is a constantly recurring and renewed experience, the distinction between reaching non-Christians versus nurturing Christians is always inexact and elusive. In fact, we must reject the whole idea that the church deals with the sacred while the secular elements of culture deal only with the nonsacred. Church and culture are bound together. "The substance of culture is religion, and the form of religion is culture."[23]

On the other hand, wherever there is an apprehension of and participation in God's revelation, there exists the church. This means the church community and its communication exist in places not normally considered by society to be the church. And that which calls itself the church often is not fulfilling the role of church, namely, to be as pure a channel of communication about God as possible.

This situation leads the church into a paradox: how can it be the most effective and "pure" channel of communication without falling into the corruption which "effectiveness" can bring, and which sin-of-pride-in-purity engenders. All the church can do is attempt to be as faithful as possible in its faltering communication attempts, and then place itself under the same judgment as that which it uses to judge the rest of society.

Even though the church today is considerably less than perfect, it nonetheless often does raise the right questions; it takes sides, and it represents a significant challenge to existing power structures. Through it, potent biblical and other religious symbols and images manage to become manifest. For example, Selma, sanctuary, and the churches in South Africa, South America, and the Philippines all have taken on powerful meaning as symbols of liberation in recent years. Above all, the church remains one of the only places in society where people still meet on a regular basis in face-to-face relationships.

But regardless of the degree of faithfulness of the church, communication about God goes on. It occurs wherever and whenever people tell what God has done in their lives—even when the word *God* is not mentioned. Jürgen Habermas frequently uses the term "unconstrained communication" to refer to that communication which is the most comprehensive possible, transcending all other interests, values, and interpretations.[24] This unconstrained communication makes possible, and in fact requires, ideological pluralism and at the same time resists attempts at ideological conformity. But it is not antireligious. Johannes Heinrichs points out that, even when the name of Jesus Christ is never mentioned, fundamental truth may be in the process of the communication.[25] The same idea is called by Paul Tillich the "latent church,"[26] by Schillebeeckx the "anonymously Christian Church,"[27] and by Gregory Baum the "Church beyond the Church."[28] Whatever the term, it is important for the Christian to identify and celebrate these moments of religious communication which occur outside the church, and within the secular culture.

Distortions of Communication

If it is true that human communication has the potential for being an instrument for both good and bad, of both reconciliation and exploitation, it becomes even more true in the case of these extensions of human communication in the mass media.

The mass media are *not* neutral tools, any more than the automobile and the washing machine are neutral. Every medium is more than just a technique of transmission. It is a synthesis of technology combined with economic, social, and political organization. Every medium therefore affects the communication process in a unique way, *entirely aside from the way a particular communicator "uses" it.* In fact, it is entirely accurate to say that the user is used *by* the medium at the same moment that the user uses the medium.

Everything that Christian doctrine teaches about original sin and the nature of humankind is eminently applicable to communication, and especially to the more potent forms of mass media. In this respect the use of mass media is no different from the use of any other form of power, and the tendency toward will-to-power and the other lessons of moral man operating in immoral society were never more apt.[29]

A number of theologians have described ways in which Christian communication can be distorted.[30] Five situations are particularly destructive to effective communication within the Christian community:

1. When loyalty to the church is substituted for loyalty to God. This happens when the church is believed because the source (church) is substituted for the message (God). The greatest distortions of this kind come when the church tries to communicate that *it* is the infallible possessor of truth.

2. When the Bible is substituted for God as an object of ultimate loyalty and faith, that is, when the authority of the Bible is substituted for the authority of God.

3. When Christology is substituted for theology, that is, love of Christ for the love of God.

4. When the church cuts itself off from its own tradition, or when that tradition is treated as something objective and final from the past, rather than as a living memory in which the community of faith actively takes part and to which they add their own life-stories.

5. When Scripture is allegorized so that it caters to the desires of people for simple solutions at the expense of faithfulness to reality, or when Scripture is taken so literally that attempts at new scriptural understanding are considered a betrayal of the original communication.

Tillich specifies four "demonries" which have great potential for distorting Christian communicating. Each demonry is a particularly powerful value in our culture which, when taken to its extreme, tends to destroy the human values in communication. They are: *rationalization,* which tends toward sterile intellectualization and robs life of its character and vitality; *estheticism,* which cuts off true communication by maintaining an esthetic distance in order to dominate, rather than to support, others; *capitalism,* which tends to depersonalize people by providing for their hedonistic needs in order to support production and consumption regardless of its human utility; and *nationalism,* which tends to make national things sacred and in doing so to create idols out of them.[31]

In concluding this theological framework for considering communication, it is important to remind ourselves that there is no way entirely to eliminate all the hindrances to successful Christian communication. There always will be distortion in one form or another. The important thing is that communicators recognize the potential dangers and distortions, and that they not succumb to the temptation to misuse communication in the guise of communicating "more effectively."

FOUR

TELEVISION'S MYTHIC WORLD

What people learn best is not what their teachers think they teach, or what their preachers think they preach, but what their cultures in fact cultivate.

George Gerbner

The fact is incontrovertible: people today live "by the media" whereas once they lived "by the book."

William Kuhns, *The Electronic Gospel* (1969)

Does Gilligan's Island Exist?

Sherwood Schwartz writes and produces a number of popular television series, including "Gilligan's Island," a comedy originated in the 1960s in which a zany group of castaways manage to survive not only shipwreck, but each other. Schwartz tells of having received, in 1964, after six or seven of "Gilligan's Island" episodes had been on the air, a visit from a Commander Doyle of the United States Coast Guard. Commander Doyle presented Schwartz with a batch of telegrams, some addressed to Hickham Field in Honolulu, some to Vandenberg Air Force Base, some to other military bases.

While the wording of the telegrams varied, they all in substance said the same thing: "For several weeks now, we have seen American citizens stranded on some Pacific island. We spend millions in foreign aid. Why not send one U.S. destroyer to rescue those poor people before they starve to death?" The telegrams were not jokes. They came from concerned citizens.

Schwartz commented on this "most extreme case of suspension of belief I ever heard of." "Who," he asked, "did these viewers think was filming the Castaways on that island? There was even a laugh track on the show. Who was laughing at the survivors of the wreck of the S.S. Minnow? It boggled my mind."[1]

There were not thousands of letters and telegrams. There were fewer than two dozen. But if some adults, even a few, believed "Gilligan's Island" was real, imagine the effect other television programs have, programs which place much greater emphasis upon reality.

The purpose of this chapter is to examine the role of television's mythic world—the world of "Gilligan's Island" and hundreds of other "places" and "people" who exist, to some degree at least, in the minds of America's viewers. This television world is important because in some ways it has become almost as tangible a map which people carry around in their heads as the map of the real world itself. And through this map, the world of television supplies the rules by which we live, or more precisely, it supplies the rules behind the rules.

Worldview: The Rules behind the Rules

What every society must have if it is to survive is *commonality*—common interests, language, tradition, institutions, values, ends. Above all, there must be a set of common assumptions—assumptions about who we are, who has the power, what we can and cannot be, what we can and cannot do.

It is the nature of these underlying assumptions to be hidden, to be embedded so deeply in the culture that they are not easily visible. When we teach children "good grammar," we really are teaching them the social structure: space/time relationships, how to solve problems, certain aspects of sexism, racism, and classism. For example, when we say "mankind must . . ." when we mean "everyone must . . .," we are making a social statement about the relative roles of men and women. Americans have only one word for "snow," but the Eskimos have more than a dozen—because snow is far more *important* to them. And the Chinese character for "trouble" is two women in the same house, which says something significant about human relations.

These hidden assumptions come to light only when we begin to ask such questions as, What are those things that we never have to ask about? What are those things that are not only true but are simply *there*? What are those things given to us in "the way things are"?

There are ways to uncover the hidden worldview. For example, studying advanced geometry is important because it makes students consider worlds quite different from the world they assume to be "true"—worlds where parallel lines meet, where the shortest distance between two points is a curved line. Science fiction, *Mad* magazine and the study of foreign languages all provide perspective on the social world in the same way—by questioning the given, the assumed reality.

Society resists this probing, this questioning of what *is*. Society needs stability, and stability depends on commonality, uniformity, conformity. Thus every society propagandizes and censors. Jacques Ellul has devoted an entire book to describing propaganda as an all-pervasive aspect of communication in every society. To Ellul, propaganda is not a plan created by the people in power to legitimate lies, but is something that grows out of the needs of the whole society and serves to sustain the society. Propaganda uses all the media of communication, but it is most effective when it reaches an individual "alone in the mass," cut off from group participation, for example, while watching TV. Propaganda tries to separate a person away from outside points of reference, such as a transcendent religious reference, in order to encourage a tunnel vision which unquestioningly accepts the society's worldview as "the way it is."[2]

In addition to propaganda, society also employs censorship over communications which threaten the commonplace values and assumptions. We are describing censorship here not in the technical sense of prior restraint on speech and enforced by governmental sanctions, but the sometimes equally effective restraints achieved by the complex web of cultural forces. Such censorship may be legal, as with laws against obscenity. It may be political, as with the press blackout during the American invasion of Grenada. It is most likely to be economic, as in the case of TV's exclusion of unusual or extreme points of view because they tend to reduce the profits of broadcasters.

Given these definitions, propaganda and censorship are not something imposed on the people by evil manipulators. They are ingrained in the normal structures of society, an ongoing and pervasive process in every society that gives the people something they want and need very badly: stability, cohesion, and common purpose.

Our society creates this commonality primarily through the mass media of communication. Every activity—games, work, play, sex, study, eating, resting, every medium—verbal, nonverbal, signs, symbols, architecture, paintings, books, memos, letters, maps, and so on, and every institution—family, school, business, church—are mediators of the culture. But only in the past 75 years have there developed the mass media of communication—the telephone, the large-volume newspaper, the wireless telegraph, the radio and television. All of these are primarily *social,* rather than technical inventions, because they have changed the speed, the extent, and the nature of the process whereby a society maintains commonality, and thus have changed the nature of society itself.

The mass media select and distort what they mediate to us, for two reasons. First, they do so because it is their nature, since they cannot possibly mediate *everything* that happens, from *all* points of view. They do so, second, because society needs the media to help create the common world of which all can be a part. This involves selection and distortion which, because it often is made unconsciously, automatically, without intention on the part of the selectors, and also because usually many individuals are involved in the selection process (writer, cameraman, director, editor, producer, distributors, sponsor, audience), it often is impossible to detect, much less to analyze or to understand.

Here we return to Ellul's concept of The Technique. The Technique is not a particular propagandist with a point of view. It is a method of solving problems, and thus is completely amoral. It asks only how best to get this done, how to solve this particular problem at this time. It does not ask what is true, or what is just or what is right. As applied to television, the only question which The Technique allows the creative people in the media industry to ask is how to reach the most people most of the time most efficiently.

The result is that television becomes extremely *attractive.* The Technique does not use fear or threats, nor is it interested in devising some kind of insidious propaganda as it was understood in the 1930s. Rather, it creates in people's minds needs and fears and hopes for which *it* can provide the answers. This way it makes people eager to buy. And in today's economy, such a powerful Technique, or propaganda, is essential. Without it, the economy simply would stop operating.

To be sure, television is a window on the world. But a window, by its very nature, selects out only a small piece of reality. And although its glass may be relatively transparent, it shuts out heat and cold, the noise and smells of the real world outside, and like the tinted glass in today's buses and airports, it may totally change the color of everything "out there." Actually, TV acts more as a filter than as a window—a filter selecting images, extracting unpleasant (and pleasant) elements, coloring others, and making a whole world seem real to us when it is in fact nothing more than thousands of bright phosphors dancing on a piece of glass.

The acculturation process which we all go through is itself something we have to learn. Psychologist Rudolf Arnheim says that a child who enters school today faces "a 12 to 20 year apprenticeship in alienation."[3] As soon as a child learns to *name* something, he or she begins to separate the self from it. And before long the child learns to handle words and concepts, but at the risk of becoming estranged from the object talked about. It finally learns to manipulate a world of words and numbers, but does not learn to experience the real world. Arnheim might well have gone on to say that exposure to television for hours every day simply adds to the separation of youngsters from the world of reality. Or, even more critically, it creates for them a *new* reality.

It also provides an optional reality for adults. Abraham Moles, director of the Social Psychology Institute at Strasbourg, points out that while TV has been a cultural life buoy for farmers, lonely people, and the culturally and the socially impoverished in France, it has at the same time been a pressure toward the banal and the constricting for those already experiencing a communication-rich life. But in both cases, as the individual is exposed to more and more TV, he or she becomes a bit less able to differentiate between the fictional universe and the real world.[4]

Television has thus become a major source of authority as to what is "real." Studs Terkel tells about the time he attended a baseball game at Wrigley Field when he saw Ron Santo strike out. A full 30 seconds after it happened, the fan next to Terkel, with his set in his hand, turned to him and said: "Santo struck out." Terkel asked him how he had found out so fast. "Lou Boudreau just announced it," came the reply. Terkel's companion had come to trust the magic box more than his own eyes.

And television literally tells us who we are, and what we are. Richard Speck, the man who in 1966 murdered eight student nurses in Chicago, recalled later that while still at large in Chicago, more than a week after committing the crime, he looked up at a TV set in a neighborhood tavern and saw there the face of O. W. Wilson, the superintendent of police. "We're looking for a man named Richard Speck," Wilson announced. It was at that moment, Speck reported, that he knew he had committed the murders. Since he had been publicly informed by the medium that he had done something, Speck knew it had to be so.

In providing this common experience of "reality," television uses the tools of myth, symbol, image, and fantasy. Myth, of course, is not used here to refer to stories of long ago or to stories we know are not true. Just the opposite. Myths are those stories that tell us who we are, what we have done, and what we can (and cannot) do. They deal with power (who has it, who doesn't), with value (what is of value and what is not), and with morality (what is right and permissible, what is forbidden). Michael Real defines mythic activity as "the collective reenactment of symbolic archetypes that express the shared emotions and ideals of a given culture."[5] He notes that Ernst Cassirer placed myth among the basic symbol systems through which humans express and control their environment.

The myths of our society constitute a kind of religious framework, providing us with a belief and value system and expressing the things we uncritically assume as *given* in our lives. The myths express, not the rules written down in our laws and in our Bibles, but the real rules, the unwritten rules—*the rules behind the rules*. In a sense, they express what is really real, what is ultimate reality—and that is another term for religion.

Myths are expressed in symbols and images that reach us less at the surface, cognitive level, than at the level of our inner fantasy world. Stanley Kubrick, creator of such memorable films as "Dr. Strangelove," "2001: A Space Odyssey," and "Barry Lyndon," understands how this happens: "I think an audience watching a film or a play is in a state very similar to dreaming, and that the dramatic experience becomes a kind of controlled dream. . . . But the important point here is that the film communicates on a subconscious level, and the audience responds to the basic shape of the story on a subconscious level, as it responds to a dream."[6] The image-symbol-fantasy level of communication is far more powerful than the cognitive level because we find it more difficult to bring these elements up to a level of consciousness where we can analyze them and talk about them in a verbal, linear, controlled, and thus nonthreatening way.

Images come to us from mother, from the churches, from the schools, and from Washington—to name a few. But mass media today provide the overwhelming input. Leo Bogart, for many years a top advertising executive, says in his book *Strategy in Advertising:*

> Every day 4.2 billion advertising messages pour forth from 1,754 daily newspapers, millions of others from 8,151 weeklies, and 1.4 billion more each day from 4,147 magazines and periodicals. There are 3,895 AM and 1,136 FM radio stations broadcasting an average of 730,000 commercials a day. And 770 television stations broadcast 100,000 commercials a day. Every day millions of people are confronted with 2,500,000 outdoor billboards, with 2,500,000 car cards and posters in buses, subways and commuter trains and with 51,300,000 direct mail pieces.[7]

Perhaps Mr. Bogart, a staunch champion of advertising, would be disappointed to learn that the ads on television, though a highly visible and controversial aspect of the mass media of communication, are only a *small part* of TV's total impact. For when we are watching television, *all* of it is massaging us, to use Marshall McLuhan's phrase, *all the time*. News, sports events, dramas, situation comedies, musicals, soap operas, documentaries, full-length feature films, even the weather report—all are providing part of the mass media's mythic world. They are all describing the roles and powers (and looks, dress, language, gestures, values, and assumptions) which all of us tend to "put on," to try out, and, in many cases, to adopt, in real life.

The Religious Functions of Television

Several observers of media have suggested that television today actually is performing many of the functions heretofore relegated to religion. Michael Real points out that much of popular culture, including television, presents *morality plays* to the public. These plays, which were based on scriptural themes and dramatized for the illiterate masses of the Middle Ages the struggle of good with evil, embodied in various players virtues such as innocence, beauty, kindness, and patriotism in their triumph over vices such as sloth, ugliness, gluttony, lying, and cheating. With the triumph of goodness over evil came "happiness" as defined by the play. Present-day TV morality plays do the same thing, defining virtues, vices, and "happiness" for today's audiences.[8]

Gregor Goethals has analyzed some of the specific religious roles television performs for our society: ritual and ceremony, such as the

Kennedy and Humphrey funerals; icons which help us articulate and shape beliefs through visual forms, such as the glorification of the machine and technology in TV commercials about speeding automobiles and washing machines turning our whiter-than-white loads of laundry; iconoclasm which attacks the status quo in the name of morality, through programs such as Edward R. Murrow's "See It Now" and today's "Sixty Minutes"; and finally, sacrament substitutes helping provide people with a sense of social experience, which are found in commercials that promise miracles and, above all, happiness (redemption from overweight, ring-around-the-collar, bad breath, or simple human loneliness).[9]

In America we are developing a new kind of liturgical year to mark the passing of the seasons, which includes the Rose Bowl Parade, Super Sunday baseball, the U.S. Open in tennis, and that key religious festival, the Super Bowl. Joseph Price suggests that the Super Bowl now signals a convergence of sports, politics, and myth—the basic elements of celebration united in many earlier cultures. In America it is accomplished through television. The invocation is a series of political rituals: the singing of the national anthem and the unfurling of a 50-yard American flag, followed by an impressive Air Force tactical squadron fly-over. The pregame program show features members from each team portrayed as superheros, demigods who not only have the skill to excel in the sport, but also to succeed in business. The coin is tossed by a member of the Football Hall of Fame (which itself is part of the new ersatz-religious world and amounts to latter-day canonization), while at the end of the game the Most Valuable Player signifies the possibility of continuing canonization in the future.

According to Price, the two dominant myths of the festival relate to our understanding of what our nation is and has been. One myth is based on the ritual action of the game itself. "The football team invades foreign land, traverses it completely, and completes the conquest by settling in the end zone. The goal is to carry the ritual object, the football, into the most hallowed area belonging to the opponent, his innermost sanctuary. There, and only there, can the ritual object touch earth without incurring some sort of penalty."

The second myth has to do with the violent nature of the game itself. "To a certain extent, football is a contemporary enactment of the American frontier spirit." But the half-time show deals with innocence—

young, scrubbed-faced girls and boys exuding cleanliness and purity. This continues the mythology that "even in our nation's history of subjugation, a sense of manifest destiny was often associated with extending our boundaries . . . [so] the people did not think they bore final responsibility for the displacement of natives or infringement on their hunting place. In other words; the assignment to God of the responsibility for territorial expansion was an attempt to maintain the illusion of blamelessness among those who forcibly took alien lands." [10]

The Media Worldview

What specifically are the mass media telling us about who we are, what we can do and be, and what is of value? Here we are looking for the symbolic meanings and the underlying myths that are far more important than the surface story line, message, or "content." While these latter are important, we must look more deeply for environment, functions, and context, and, most important of all, for human relationships that define social roles and tell us who has power, who is aggressor, and who is victim. We must read the TV "text" for its basic cultural meaning.

Consider who populates this television world, keeping in mind that for most Americans, this TV world becomes *their world* at least three hours a day, every day, through most of their lives. George Gerbner's research at the Annenberg School of Communications in Philadelphia tells us that in the TV world two-thirds to three-fourths of the important characters are male, American, middle class, unmarried, and in the prime of life—and they are the people who run the world. Although about half of TV-land characters are married, among TV teachers, only 18% of the women and 20% of the men are married. [11] Furthermore, the women "find themselves, and a man" by *leaving* teaching. Failure in love and life is a requisite for success in teaching, and the problems of TV teachers are solved by leaving their profession—not by towns raising taxes, building schools, or giving higher salaries. On the other hand, TV journalists are strong and honest. And TV scientists are deceitful, cruel, and dangerous; their research leads to murder in fully half the situations.

Violence on TV, unlike real-life violence, rarely occurs between people who know each other well, and most of it does not result from rage, hate, despair, or panic, but from the businesslike pursuit of personal gain, power, or duty. Fully one-third of TV's violent people, according to Gerbner, could be considered "professionals" in the business of violence.

Marriage seems to shrink men and to make them unfit for the free-wheeling, powerful, and violent life-style of "real" men. On the other hand, women appear to *gain* power through marriage, though they lose some of their capacity for violence.

White, young Americans are more than twice as likely as all others to commit lethal violence and then live to reach a happy ending. In the symbolic shorthand of TV, the free and strong kill in a cause that was good to begin with.

Thus there is an interesting trade-off in the TV world. The price of being good (such as a teacher) is powerlessness. The price of having power (such as a scientist) is to be evil. But if one happens to be a powerful, white American, then the end justifies all kinds of means, and one is rewarded with the TV images of happiness.

In a complex society such as ours, it would be impossible to detail all of the images and symbols that go into creating its commonality. However, there are a few central myths and values from which most of the images and symbols spring:

1. *The fittest survive.* According to sociologist Marie Augusta Neal, the major myth of our Western culture is the social Darwinian theory initiated by Herbert Spencer—the concept that between ethnic groups there exist genetic differences large enough to justify programming for unequal natural capacities for responsible decision making, specifically in the interests of the group one represents. Social Darwinism dominates our policy-making regarding education, jobs, geographical residential allotments, provisions for recreation, health services, and the uses of human beings to carry on wars.

It is no accident that in Gerbner's TV-violence profile, lower class and nonwhite characters are especially prone to victimization, are more violent than their middle class counterparts, and pay a high price for engaging in violence (jail, death).[12] As our myth suggests, the fittest survive, and the fittest in our media worldview are *not* lower class, nonwhite Americans.

2. *Power and decision making start at the center and move out.* In the media world, the political word comes from Washington, the financial word comes from New York, and the entertainment word comes from Hollywood. While watching television, one gets the sense of

personally existing at the edge of a giant network where someone at the center pushes the right button and instantaneously millions of us "out there" see what has been decided we will see.

Of course, there are alternatives to the worldview that power should move from the center to the edges. Our own Declaration of Independence proposes just the opposite—that government derives its power from the consent of the governed, in other words, that the flow of power should be from the periphery to the center. But the opposite model is much more supportive of the needs of the industrial revolution, the rise of a major nation-state and the demands of the new technological era. Center-out clearly is essential to the maintenance of both our centralized governmental bureaucracy and our capitalist economy.

In our society, people at the center make decisions about what the others need and what they get. Mass production means standardization: whether people want it or not, the items on the shelves of our supermarkets become more and more the same, while mass advertising convinces us that we are getting more and more diversity. Ten different boxes of detergent. Twenty versions of wheat cereal. Five varieties of aspirin.

The idea that people in the power center should plan for others extends into corporate offices, national church bureaucracies, and social welfare agencies. The result is that corporate business leaders wonder why they are so low in the credibility polls, church leaders wonder why they are losing their jobs and why their budgets are shrinking, and social workers wonder why the poor don't appreciate the plans that have been worked out for them.

3. *Happiness consists of limitless material acquisition.* This myth has several corollaries.

One is that *consumption is inherently good*—a concept driven home effectively by the advertising industry. Another is that *property, wealth, and power are more important than people.* We need only consider the vast following for Ronald Reagan's proposition that the Panama Canal is ours because we bought and paid for it to see how far this myth has made its way into our consciousness. We did, after all, pay for the Canal Zone. The fact that our control of the canal today results in depriving the people of Panama of their human rights is regrettable, but a deal is a deal. Or recall the riots during the late 1960s. It was when looters started to take things from the stores that the police started to kill. Both human life and property may be sacred, but, in our media worldview, property rights are just a little more sacred.

4. *Progress is an inherent good.* At one level this myth is symbolized by the words "new and improved" attached every few years to every old product. But the myth goes much deeper. Lewis Mumford believes that the "premise underlying this whole age, its capitalist as well as its socialist development, has been 'the doctrine of Progress.'" Progress, he writes, "was [like] a tractor that laid its own roadbed and left no permanent imprint of its own track, nor did it move toward an imaginable and humanly desirable destination." Rather, *"the going is the goal"*—not because there is any inherent beauty of usefulness in going, but because to stop going, to stop wasting, to stop consuming more and more, to say at any given moment that "enough is enough" would spell immediate doom.[13] This myth is essential to the support of The Technique's value that "what works is good" and that what is important is the successful solving of problems, not the question of goals.

5. *There exists a free flow of information.* Of course the whole import of this analysis is that instead of a genuine free flow of information, there is consistent, pervasive, and effective propaganda and censorship as we have defined them after Jacques Ellul. Such a view is resisted most of all by the men and women who spend their careers reporting the news. But they are the very ones least able to judge the matter, for they were selected and trained by the system so that they could be depended upon to operate within its assumptions and myths. When was the last time you saw a long-haired, radical hippy anchoring the evening TV news? Although the example may appear bizarre, the point is not: radical, or even nonestablishment, points of view have almost no opportunity to find expression in mass television.

This is not to condemn newsmen and newswomen any more than others of us who function uncritically within the system year in and year out. When Walter Cronkite used to say, "And that's the way it is," he was summing up the way *we* feel about the information our society wants and needs to hear every day.

What are the values that the mass media communicate to us on behalf of our culture? *Power* heads the list: power over others; power over nature. As Hannah Arendt pointed out, in today's media world it is not so much that power corrupts as that the aura of power, its glamorous trappings, attracts.[14]

Close to power are the values of *wealth* and *property,* the idea that *everything can be purchased* and that *consumption* is an intrinsic good. The values of *narcissism,* of *immediate gratification* of wants, and of *creature comforts* follow close behind.

Thus the mass-media worldview tells us that we are basically good, that happiness is the chief end of life, and that happiness consists in obtaining material goods. The media transform the value of sexuality into sex appeal, the value of self-respect into pride, the value of will-to-live into will-to-power. They exacerbate acquisitiveness into greed; they deal with insecurity by generating more insecurity, and anxiety by generating more anxiety. They change the value of recreation into competition and the value of rest into escape. And perhaps worst of all, the media constrict our experience and substitute media world for real world so that we become less and less able to make the fine value-judgments that living in such a complex world requires.

Within society, the media are the obedient servants of the economic system. The high technology required for our current mass communication system, with its centralized control, its high profits, its capital-intensive nature, and its ability to reach every individual in the society immediately and economically, makes it perfectly suited for a massive production-consumption system that is equally centralized, profitable, and capital-intensive. In fact, our current production-consumption system in the United States simply could not *exist* without a communication system that trains people to be knowledgeable, efficient, and hard-working producers and consumers. The fact that the capitalist system tends to turn everything into a commodity is admirably suited to the propaganda system of the mass media which turns each member of the audience into a consumer.

In terms of the political system, the media, again reflecting the values held by society generally, give us politics by image, with politicians and their campaigns treated as products to be sold rather than as ideas to be understood. The whole media approach to the war in Vietnam was guided by the necessity of a superpower to create for itself an image that would convince the world—and itself—that it was number one, the mightiest power on earth (our most important value). The invasion of Grenada and the bombing of Libya were handled the same way to support the same value.

The media handling of Watergate is revealing in this regard. The public and the media were shocked not so much by what the president and his men *did* as by the fact that they got caught, publicly, in a way that could not be imaged away. And after Watergate we saw the immediate return to the old value-system. Those indicted and convicted were overwhelmed with lucrative offers from publishers and television to tell their stories, thus once again driving home the point that our society demands "positive" images, including even more lies and fabrications, in order to mitigate the horror of the cover-up, to rehabilitate the criminals in the American TV viewer's eyes, and, above all, to help restore through imagery the public's confidence in the political system.

The Christian Worldview

Christianity has its own worldview, its own vision of who people are and are not, of what they can and cannot do, and what is of value and what is not. The task of the Christian has always been to evaluate and understand the historical order in terms of the eternal order, to learn how to live within the present world and yet not be of it, to discern both the signs of the times and the signs of God's kingdom. But to do this today requires understanding and evaluating the current media, and television in particular, from a Christian perspective. It requires theological analysis.

I am not overstating the case to say that theological analysis of media is one of the most important tasks of American Christians today. Individuals need to cultivate the ability to stand back and create aesthetic and intellectual "distance" between themselves and what they see on TV, and then, from a critical perspective informed by their own faith, look at what TV is doing and saying.

Unless we achieve and maintain this "distance," we easily become victims of our own ignorance and complacency. The world of television easily becomes our world. On the other hand, if we develop a stance of critical reflection, we can both clarify our own value system and search back to find the roots of our faith. This moving back and forth between faith and practice, between spirit and reality, between kingdom of God and the kingdoms of this world, is precisely the calling of all who today consider themselves religious.

This kind of theological analysis is not really so difficult. It is rooted in the Bible, in the history of the church, and in personal reflection.

And it certainly is too important to be left to the professional theologians! What it requires is a reasonable amount of biblical literacy and a determination to be completely honest.

The place to begin is with the great themes of the Bible:

● *The creation story.* The Old Testament begins with an affirmation of the goodness of God's creation. Genesis affirms the value of human guidance and transformation of nature in harmony with the whole of creation, and it rejects our culture's frequent affirmation of consumption and waste. Genesis also affirms the fundamental value of each human life, our essential equality as human beings, and our interrelatedness with nature, rather than television's view that young, white, unmarried males are somehow given a position of power considerably "above" females, older people, and minorities.

● *The fall.* The recognition that evil comes into the world through the self-centeredness of individuals is a strong corrective to television's frequent appeals to narcissism, to self-glorification and instant gratification.

● *The covenant story.* Reconciliation takes place after the fall, after alienation and pride and selfishness have separated humanity from God's will. God blessing Abraham and his tribe affirms that God will be with all humanity if they worship the true God and not other less-than-God gods. This means that the worship of anything that is less than God—possessions, power, beauty, success—is a sin. Yet these are the very things glorified (worshiped?) in the world of television.

● *The kingdom of God.* Jesus taught that the kingdom of God is within us, not something "out there." It is present in the spirit, waiting for women and men to testify to its presence and power in their lives. It also is present in hope for the future, in the expression of that to which we should strive in the face of seemingly impossible odds in the real world. Much of television, on the other hand, proposes a world without spirit, without hope—a world in which literally everything, and everyone, can be bought.

● *The servant and Savior.* Jesus is both servant and Savior, who through his death and resurrection becomes the Lord of history, providing both reconciliation and hope to all in the future. This is a key image which guides both the Christian's personal life and the church's life. The television image is that consumption is the guide to both personal and corporate life.

A number of specific values emerge from this biblical view. Through Amos God calls for justice and righteousness (Amos 5:21-24). Through Micah he requires kindness and humility (Mic. 6:8). And through Isaiah he demands that we correct oppression (Isaiah 42–43).

Instead of television's affirmation of wealth and possessions, Jesus tells the rich young ruler to sell all that he has and to follow his way. He makes it clear that wealth has the same chance of entering the kingdom of God as a rope has of threading a needle (Luke 18:18-23).

As for television's assumption that money can buy anything, Jesus tells the story of the wealthy man who decided to build a bigger barn, but then suddenly died, so Jesus asks, "What does a man gain by winning the whole world at the cost of his true self?" (Mark 8:36 NEB). In contrast to television's affirmation of the ultimate value of creature comforts and self-gratification, Jesus affirms that if anyone wants to be a follower he must leave self-centeredness behind and follow him, which involves taking up the cross (Matt. 16:24).

In contrast to television's worldview that we are basically good, that happiness is the chief end of life and that happiness consists of obtaining material goods, the Christian worldview holds that human beings are susceptible to the sin of pride and will-to-power, that the chief end of life is to glorify God and enjoy him forever, and that happiness consists in creating the kingdom of God within one's self and among one's neighbors.

Communication as Incarnation

In addition to these biblical themes and values, the whole thrust of Christian theology is that God's communication is incarnation. God is not an idea, an ideal, somebody "out there." We do not live in two worlds—a "good" world and a "bad" world. *God is with us.* Whoever understands this understands the Almighty. Among other things, it means that we must learn to love the world we find ourselves in, and this includes television. But it also means that we live in hope that God will make right what is wrong in the world, and this also includes television. Incarnational theology has important implications for what television tries to teach us.

God's revelation through real people and events signifies that genuine meaning must be related to the life histories of actual individuals. If actual individuals must be involved, then communication must be *two-way,* dialogic, because the only way to understand and to know other people is to listen, more than to speak. Also, if life histories are involved, then communication must be a continuous *process*, rather than a single event. It must be open to input from both listener and speaker, and it must of necessity be full of the *ambiguity* and uncertainty that characterizes the human condition.

This kind of communication—two-way, ambiguous, in-process—stands in marked contrast to the "hypodermic needle" model that characterizes the communication of TV and most other mass media. To repeat what we have said earlier, commercial television simply is not designed to maximize communication. It is designed to maximize sales. It is structured to meet the needs of the sponsors, not the needs of the audience. Therefore, communication is one-way, and individuals in the audience are treated as things to be "influenced" in ways that have nothing to do with their needs or their life histories.

Clearly, we find ourselves living in a society which through its most powerful medium communicates a set of values, assumptions, and worldview which are completely at odds with the religious values, assumptions, and worldview professed by more than 70% of its citizens. The next question we must ask is how religion itself, and the Christian church in particular, have responded to this challenge. One of the most powerful and controversial responses of the last two decades has been that of the electronic church, and it is to this response that we now turn.

FIVE

THE ELECTRONIC CHURCH AND ITS MESSAGE

Not every one who says to me, "Lord, Lord," shall enter the kingdom of heaven, but he who does the will of my Father who is in heaven.

(Matt. 7:21)

Awakenings and Revivals in America

The 1970s and 1980s in America saw the flowering of the electronic church on both radio and TV. In 1980 *Time* magazine devoted one entire "Religion" section to "Stars of the Cathode Church," depicting "the continuing drama of TV-radio preaching, one of the most successful and controversial enterprises in American religion." The article described how the "billion dollar industry" was opposed by many local pastors who feared "that with worship-by-tube, the living room sofa is supplanting the pew and gifts mailed to televangelists are taking the place of Sunday offerings." It quoted the assertion of National Religious Broadcasters' Ben Armstrong that broadcasting is shifting power from the clergy to the layman "with his hand on the dial. . . . It is a change in the power structure of American religion."[1]

Understanding in some depth the phenomenon of the electronic church is one of the best ways to understand the dilemmas confronting religion in our culture. For while the use of the new electronic technology is new, in many ways these ministries are the extension of a religious response that is older than America itself. They are part of the Great Awakenings—that series of religious responses to changes in American society whose roots reach back to a time prior to the founding of the nation.

William G. McLoughlin in his study of the Great Awakenings points out that they have been shaping American culture from its inception. He identifies four periods of Great Awakenings in our history, plus the one in which we find ourselves today: the Puritan Awakening, 1610–1740; the First Great Awakening (in America), 1730–1760; the Second Great Awakening, 1800–1830; the Third Great Awakening, 1890–1920, and the Fourth Great Awakening, 1960–1990(?).[2]

McLoughlin shows that awakenings are not merely periods of intense religious activity and reexamination, but instead are times of a fundamental intellectual reorientation of the entire American belief system and worldview. Each awakening has occurred during a period of profound cultural disorientation, when the whole cultural system was jarred by disjunctions between old beliefs and new realities, past norms and present experience, dying patterns and emerging patterns of behavior. The period which spawns a Great Awakening is a time when the realities of life in society have deviated so far from their moral and religious understandings that the authority of the old institutions are questioned. It is a time when

> the churches do not offer solace and acceptance of the prevailing order; the schools cannot maintain discipline over their pupils; the police and courts cannot maintain orderly processes of action (they often infringe the very laws they are supposed to enforce); the hospitals cannot cure; the jails burst at their seams; and, finally, the government itself fails to function with the respect and authority it requires. Political rebellion in the streets and schismatic behavior in churches create civil and ecclesiastical disorder, to which the authorities in church and state can react only by more sanctions, more censures, more punishments.[3]

Some degree of cultural stress is normal in any society. But there are times when the stresses become abnormal, when the populace truly is at odds with each other, when people cannot agree on the proper measures for coping with dangers and problems, when they blame those in authority and flout the establishment by unpatriotic acts.

Such a situation signals the need for major cultural reorientation, and this signals the beginning of a cultural awakening. Each awakening has extended for at least a full generation, perhaps more—a 30- to 40-year period. It is not a time of neurosis, although considerable cultural confusion results; rather it is a time of revitalization. It is a time when new leaders emerge who articulate a set of commonly shared beliefs and understandings—a new worldview—which the vast majority of the population accept because it makes sense in terms of their own experience, regardless of their particular denomination or religion or formal belief or affiliation.

Each of our Great Awakenings has brought about major changes in our cultural orientation. The First Great Awakening (1730–1760) made the 13 colonies into a cohesive unit by inspiring them to believe that they were, "and of right ought to be," a free and independent people, thus setting the stage for the revolution from Great Britain. The Second Great Awakening (1800–1830), coming shortly after the Constitution had launched the republic, defined what it meant to be "an American," and what was the manifest destiny of the new nation. The Third Great Awakening (1890–1920) followed a few years after the Civil War, and it helped us come to terms with the demands of science and industrial progress which were then shattering the old worldview, and led us to a liberal optimism which resulted in our attempt "to make the world safe for democracy" through two world wars.

McLoughlin suggests that the Fourth Great Awakening began about 1960, following the undeclared war in Vietnam, and that it has appeared at a time when once again we are seeking a new understanding of who we are, how we relate to the scientific worldview, and what is the meaning of the many domestic and worldwide crises that threaten our security, our sense of order, and our self-image as a mighty and righteous world power.

Each awakening has followed a similar pattern. The beginning is a period of individual stress, when people lose their bearings, become psychically or physically ill, break out in violence against family, friends, and authority, or become apathetic and incapable of functioning. People may destroy themselves by alcohol, drugs, or suicide. Families come apart, children are abused.

At this point there always arise a number of *traditionalist movements*, attempts by those with rigid personalities or with much at stake in the old order to insist that the solution to the current disorder is to adhere more strictly to the old beliefs, values, and behavior patterns. These traditionalist movements stress a return to the "old time religion," "the ways of our fathers," and "respect for the flag." They mistake symptoms for causes. They find scapegoats upon whom to project our national fears (witches in the 18th century, foreigners in the 19th, communists and atheists in the 20th).

This is in accord with sociologist Anthony F. C. Wallace's view that "rigid persons apparently prefer to tolerate high levels of chronic stress rather than make systematic changes," preferring to look backward to the "golden period" when the worldview and the social system worked; they insist it will work again if people will only conform to the old standards.[4]

In the final stage of each awakening, the traditionalists have polarized the alternatives, the traditional alternatives themselves are rejected by most of the populace, new leaders emerge who articulate a new and generally accepted worldview, and the society begins to rebuild its institutions.

This pattern in the Great Awakenings is important because in each one there has been a strong religious revival movement. I believe that the electronic church movement must be understood as part of a developing Great Awakening that is under way in America today.

Today's pattern becomes clear if we view it in light of the pattern in the previous awakenings. The First Great Awakening was heralded by spontaneous and emotional conversion experiences, scattered throughout the colonies. Soon massive and continuous revival meetings were being kept in motion by traveling preachers who were some of the best-informed and most effective communicators of their day. People began to understand that their experience in the New World had opened up an enormous gap between them and Great Britain with its king, their royal father, who refused to grant them freedom and maturity.

At this point a number of traditionalists reacted to the new demands for freedom, characterizing them as the work of the devil, and in some cases urging withdrawal into communities of the perfected saints to preserve a "saving remnant" from God's wrath as the world came to an end. But eventually the determination to throw off all authority—except God's—won the day, which resulted in a new political concept of government and of the public good: the duty of the government was to restrain the selfishness of the individual for the sake of the common good. Regeneration, republicanism, and revolution blended to set the stage for American withdrawal from the authority of British tyranny and the establishment of a new commonwealth.

The Second Great Awakening came after the American revolution had created great anticipation for the future, but that future was not being realized. Missionary work on the frontier was carried out by uneducated preachers who, in the eyes of many, were incapable of preaching true religion or restraining the wild passions of the rough, unruly frontier folk. Early in this awakening there appeared the new traditionalist movement, led by Timothy Dwight, who preached return to the old order, aroused the populace against the dangers of foreigners, attacked deistic heresies and rebellion among the youth, and urged maintaining the old establishment of religion. But the traditionalist view lost the day, with the result that the new religious orientation included the separation of church and state (Jefferson and Madison), a democratic faith in the common person (Jacksonian democracy), and acceptance of a new romanticism which brought about a flourishing of the first truly national literature, art, and architecture.

The Third Great Awakening of 1890-1920 began during a time of grave social tension. Slavery was still an issue, there was widespread unemployment and labor agitation, corruption ruled the big cities, Darwinism was attacking the laws of creation, Freud was laying bare the human psyche, and liberal Christians were attacking the uniqueness of the Christian religion. Into this crisis came a number of revivalists, but none so creative and dynamic as Billy Sunday.

Sunday led the traditionalist attack. He was the champion of "the old-time religion" and the evangelical beliefs of the 19th century. He rejected Darwinism and evolution, attacked the new naturalism and the liberal religionists, and denounced the influx of "new immigrants" (by which he meant those from eastern and southern Europe) as subverting the American way of life. But Sunday also was aware of the social ills of his day. He devoted a great deal of time to the problems of alcoholism, and in one revival city after another he succeeded in destroying the grip of the city bosses and in cleaning up corruption.

Once again, however, the traditionalist movement was rejected. The final result was the rejection within mainstream culture of biblical literalism with its repudiation of history, geology, and the scientific method, and an acceptance of the contributions of science, of evolution and Freudian psychology, of a "higher criticism" of the Bible, of the move from an agrarian economy to an industrial economy and its need for high technology, and of a rearrangement of political views to accommodate social planning and reform which became known in the churches as the Social Gospel.

By 1960 liberalism had begun to fail the expectations of the people for a better life. Once again America was plunged into a crisis because the cultural worldview did not explain what was happening in experience. The ferment of the 60s produced a challenge to our belief system that was perhaps the most drastic in our national history. Nuclear catastrophe seemed ever more likely. The Vietnam War brought with it serious doubts about our mission in the world and our credibility as a nation. The "Death of God" movement raised questions about the bankruptcy of our present churches and their religious systems. The welfare state, which grew out of the liberal movement, was full of corruption and had failed to meet its goals. Thus began the Fourth Great Awakening, which continues today.

Into this situation, right on schedule, there came the traditionalist response. The movement this time has been characterized by a revivalist campaign perhaps unparalleled in its vitality and pervasiveness, for its leaders had a new and more powerful tool than any of their predecessors—the electronic magic of radio and television.

The Beginnings of Religious Broadcasting

The first religious program was broadcast less than two months after the first licensed commercial station went on the air. On January 2, 1921, station KDKA in Pittsburgh provided a remote broadcast from Calvary Episcopal Church. The Rev. Edwin Jan van Etten, the assistant minister, spoke because the rector of the church was too busy.

Within a short time ministers across America seized upon the radio medium as an evangelistic tool. In 1923, Walter A. Maier, a professor of Old Testament at the Lutheran Church–Missouri Synod's Concordia Seminary in St. Louis, wrote an editorial entitled, "Why Not a Lutheran Broadcasting Station?" and on December 14, 1924, KFUO ("Keep Forward, Upward, Onward") became the first religious station, broadcasting from the seminary's attic.

By 1925 some 63 stations were owned by church institutions. But the rise of commercial broadcasting made frequencies increasingly valuable, and many churches were persuaded to sell them to commercial entrepreneurs, in many cases accepting a promise of free broadcast time as part of the transaction. By the 1930s the rash of church-owned stations had all but vanished. But the broadcast of Sunday services, either from church premises or station studios, had become common.

Stations and networks—the National Broadcasting Company, formed in 1926, and Columbia Broadcasting System, in 1927—faced a thorny problem as the radio evangelism spread. Which churches, groups, or sects should or could be accommodated? Broadcasters encouraged the formation of local and regional councils of churches to help them cope with this issue. On the national level the Federal (later National) Council of the Churches of Christ represented more than a score of denominations.

The councils tended to be dominated by the mainline Protestant denominations; groups and individual preachers not favored by the arrangements began to seek access by buying time on a commercial basis. At first CBS welcomed such purchases, selling network time to the Lutheran Church–Missouri Synod as well as to the fiery Father Charles E. Coughlin of the Shrine of the Little Flower in Royal Oak, Michigan. But as Father Coughlin's broadcasts turned highly political and sometimes seemed anti-Semitic, CBS adopted the NBC policy of refusing to sell time for religious purposes, instead apportioning a limited amount of free time to major Protestant, Catholic, and Jewish faith groups. Those who were bypassed, or not satisfied with their allotments, increasingly focused on local coverage, free or purchased, and in some cases organized ad hoc hookups of stations via leased telephone lines. Many made over-the-air appeals to help them continue to expand their radio evangelism.[5]

When the Communications Act was being debated in 1934, an amendment was proposed by Senators Wagner and Hatfield which would have allocated 25% of the broadcast frequencies for the exclusive use of nonprofit groups.[6] Broadcasters were furious at this proposal from educators, religious groups, farm agencies, and other nonprofit organizations, and during hearings they assured the senators that they— the broadcasters—had provided ample opportunities for such groups in the past, and that they could be trusted to continue to do so in the future. The Wagner/Hatfield Amendment was voted down, but not before Congress wrote into the bill Section 307(c), a mandate to the newly created Federal Communications Commission:

> The Commission shall study the proposal that Congress by statute

allocate fixed percentages of radio broadcasting facilities to particular types or kinds of non-profit radio programs, or to persons identified with particular types or kinds of non-profit activities and shall report to Congress, not later than February 1, 1935, its recommendations together with the reasons for the same.[7]

The FCC set hearings on the matter as one of its first orders of business, and in January of 1935 recommended that, since the broadcasters were making their facilities available in a spirit of "unity and cooperation," no fixed percentages of broadcast facilities should be allocated by Congress for the use of nonprofit activities. However, the report said:

> In order for non-profit organizations to obtain the maximum service possible, cooperation in good faith by the broadcasters is required. Such cooperation should, therefore, be under the direction of the Commission.[8]

Thus religious leaders and the other nonprofit groups did not get their frequency allocations, but they were told that the FCC would make certain that broadcasters would continue to give them time to be heard on the commercial stations.

In most cases, Protestant religious broadcasting continued to be handled through religious advisory committees of the networks, which looked to the Federal Council of Churches, which later became the National Council of Churches, the representative agency for Protestant denominations. However, some denominations and independent evangelists not related to the Federal Council purchased time from non-network stations. The Lutheran Church–Missouri Synod began syndicating "The Lutheran Hour" in 1930. The Seventh-Day Adventist Church began its radio broadcasts in 1924, and its first regularly scheduled program, "The Voice of Prophecy," in 1930. Several Roman Catholic dioceses and orders, and hundreds of local preachers sought time on local radio. Independents such as Charles E. Fuller, Aimee Semple McPherson, M. R. De Haan and H. M. S. Richards put most of their funds into buying time. By 1933, conventional Protestant broadcasting accounted for only 28% of the total religious radio output.[9]

A basic policy difference developed among religious broadcasters. The larger, established, mainline denominations generally held the view that broadcasters should provide time on the air for a balanced presentation of religious views, roughly representing the proportion of various religious groups in the community, even if this required stations to supply the time without charge, and that this was consistent with the understandings reached between Congress and the broadcasters when the allocation of nonprofit stations was defeated. The smaller, more sect-type groups believed that they were being ignored, and accused the cooperative groups of attempting to silence them, even though the networks set aside some free time for them. They chose to purchase time and to make financial appeals over the air.

After World War II, with the rise of television, the American networks emphasized a policy of "cooperative broadcasting." The major faith groups were invited to provide assistance to the networks in the production of weekly half-hour television series dedicated to religion, such as NBC's "Frontiers of Faith" and CBS's "Look Up and Live." The American Broadcasting Company, split off from NBC in 1943, was represented by "Directions."

A wide diversity of groups maintained a presence on radio and television. The Mormons were represented on network radio (first NBC, then CBS) by a nondoctrinal musical program, "Music and the Spoken Word," featuring the Tabernacle Choir. The Seventh-Day Adventists were represented by "The Voice of Prophecy," begun in 1930. In 1945 the Jewish Theological Seminary of America started "The Eternal Light," offered weekly over NBC radio and occasionally on television. Some groups sought to extend their coverage through program syndication—the United Methodists with "The Way," the Lutheran Church–Missouri Synod with "This Is the Life." Many Catholic groups were program producers, including the Paulist Productions' "Insight" series, the Franciscans' syndicated radio dramas on the lives of the saints, and later a series of television spots. Commercial sponsorship became a factor when Texaco sponsored Monsignor Fulton J. Sheen in "Life Is Worth Living," on Dumont and ABC television. In 1968 the U.S. Catholic Conference established an Office of Radio and Television to represent it in all broadcasting matters. For 30 years, TV network audiences for the mainline programs ranged as high as 15 million viewers per week. All three faith groups maintained weekly network radio programs as well.

But, as the FCC became increasingly lax in its congressional mandate to insure that "non-profit organizations obtain the maximum service possible," individual evangelists discovered the power of broadcasting—and television in particular—and they began to purchase the better quality time which broadcasters were reluctant to provide churches as a public service. The major pioneer in television evangelism was Billy Graham.

Characteristics of the Electronic Church

Where Billy Sunday's revivals left off, Billy Graham's picked up. In many ways, Graham is the spiritual descendant of Sunday. Both grew up in fundamentalist homes. Both experienced powerful personal conversions. Both had a gift for pulse-quickening oratory. Both burned with a sense of mission. Both felt the world was headed for imminent catastrophe. Both were convinced that they must first save individual souls, and that social reforms would follow. Both were backed by rich and powerful men—Sunday by John D. Rockefeller, Graham by William Randolph Hearst. Both innovated communication techniques that startled the world— Sunday with his elaborate teams of "experts" and sophisticated and expensive "revival machinery" that developed huge audiences; Graham with his even more impressive cadre of technicians, and his use of television to extend his reach beyond the wildest dreams of earlier evangelists. Using these innovative techniques, both achieved success—in fact, far more income and power than any other previous evangelists.

Sunday and Graham also shared essentially the same theology: a fundamentalism that urged a return to basics—the Bible, the family, hard work and clean living, and simple belief in God's power. They attacked many of the same social ills—alcohol, sloth, swearing, crime, adultery, communism. They attacked the same religious perspectives— liberalism, the Social Gospel, higher criticism of the Bible, and, to some degree, Roman Catholicism. They possessed a similar preaching style—Bible in hand, striding about the stage, completely self-assured and filled with authority, speaking in plain terms to the masses without much thought to structure or logic, presenting an image both dynamic and convincing.

Billy Graham's message and timing fit perfectly into the traditionalist reaction which has come with each Great Awakening. He appealed to the growing personal alienation, the sense of nuclear doom, and the international disillusionment that characterized the postwar era. The solution he proposed was a return to the traditional Christian imagery and rules, coupled with a strong emphasis on law and order. His success to no small degree was due to the support he garnered among the wealthy and the captains of industry who found in Graham the perfect carrier of the Puritan values of hard work, clean living, and individual morality. His endorsement of the social status quo and the dominant power structure endeared him to the nation's political and economic elites.

Billy Graham had one thing which Billy Sunday never possessed: the ability to reach millions of persons directly, immediately, and visually, through television. Because of his message and his technique, together with the growing dominance of the world created by television, Graham became far more of a national celebrity than any of his predecessors. Whereas Sunday once met with President Wilson during World War I, Graham was the welcomed guest and spiritual advisor of Presidents Eisenhower, Nixon, and, to some extent, Johnson and Ford. Whereas Sunday was a known name in America, Graham became a celebrity in much of Europe, Asia, Africa, and Latin America as well.

But Billy Graham was only the avant-garde of the electronic-church movement. Many were right behind him. In fact, in terms of style and technique, we already have seen four generations of electronic-church preachers, and a fifth is on the way.

Graham represented the first generation. By the 1950s he had brought television cameras and sophisticated advertising techniques to his mass meetings and, with the help of Hearst's newspapers, became an overnight success. His technique was relatively simple. It depended primarily on generating massive rallies, and the TV cameras were brought in to *cover* the rallies as they might cover a football game or a political assembly.

The second generation, in terms of style and technique, was Oral Roberts. Roberts was originally a tent evangelist who began to buy radio time. But he quickly saw the power of television and by the mid-1950s had the idea of bringing the cameras right into the tent so that the cameras (and the audience) began to *participate* in his preaching and healing sessions. Roberts even offered to heal people right in their homes if they would place their hands on the TV set. Inevitably, as television began to spread his fame, the medium began to take control of the tent meetings themselves, until finally Roberts moved out of the tent and into a formal TV studio setting.

The third generation developed in the 1960s, when Rex Humbard, another early tent evangelist, built the first church designed expressly for television. "The Cathedral of Tomorrow" in Akron, Ohio, came complete with a 360° rotating stage with risers, like a huge revolving birthday cake, on which the entire Humbard family could stand and sing "God Is Love" while the cameras picked out first Rex, then "Our Mom" Maude, and finally all their children and grandchildren, clothed in color-coordinated pastel suits and dresses. The entire "service" was basically a *TV production*.

The fourth generation of the electronic ministries is best exemplified by Pat Robertson and "The 700 Club." Robertson, son of the late U.S. Senator A. Willis Robertson of Virginia and a graduate of Yale Law School, failed the New York bar exam, then attended New York Theological Seminary and tried starting a ghetto ministry in New York City before moving back to Virginia. He bought a tiny defunct UHF station in Portsmouth, Va., for $70 in 1959, and over the next 20 years perfected a 90-minute format which closely resembles the most popular commercial TV *host-show* programs.[10]

His program, "The 700 Club," got its name from one of the television fund-raising marathons he developed in the early days of his ministry. In terms of style, not only had the tent and stadium disappeared from "The 700 Club," but the program's elements were almost indistinguishable from those of the "Tonight Show," with a genial host (Robertson), a foil with whom the host could banter (Ben Kinchlow, who now has become a "co-host"), guests lounging around a coffee table, musical breaks with cut-aways to commercials (for mission projects and CBN membership) and a "studio audience" to applaud and laugh.

The fifth generation of electronic-church programming has recently emerged, and it represents a complete departure from the old formats. Pat Robertson, with his enormous cash flow and no stockholders, has had sufficient funds to put together a *genuine TV network*, feeding some 5500 cable systems nationwide via satellite on a 24-hour-a-day basis. This CBN Network program service consists of "family" programming, including "The 700 Club" (broadcast twice each day) and "Christian commercials." Many of the shows are reruns of family-oriented fare from the 1960s ("The Flying Nun," "Hazel," "Father Knows Best," "Wagon Train," "Gunsmoke") and old game shows ("Name That Tune," "Tic Tac Dough").

The development from the first generation of religious-TV evangelism to the fifth is a development from covering the old-style rallies of Billy Graham to a format and style which has become less and less distinguishable from secular commercial television. It remains to be seen whether the fifth generation, a commercial network, will crowd out the first four because the audience is basically interested more in simple TV with less sex and violence than the present fare, or whether the old evangelical styles will continue to appeal to many of the audience precisely because they tune to the electronic-church programs to get away from commercial TV and return to "the old-time religion." The most likely scenario is that the latest "religious" programming will only segment further the audience in an already-crowded field.

The total audience for electronic-church programs peaked in 1977, when the weekly audience for the top 10 TV evangelists ranged from 423,000 for James Robison to 3.9 million for Oral Roberts. Audiences dropped after that, although Pat Robertson's "700 Club" has increased its share through the cable systems which were fed via satellite by the Christian Broadcasting Network (CBN).

The following were the top-rated electronic-church programs, as of November 1986, according to the A. C. Nielsen report:[11]

Program	Households
1. "The Hour of Power" (Robert Schuller)	1.27 million
2. Jimmy Swaggart	1.05 million
3. Oral Roberts	814,000
4. "The World Tomorrow" (World Wide Church of God)	560,000
5. "The Day of Discovery" (Radio Bible Class)	449,000
6. "The Old-Time Gospel Hour" (Jerry Falwell)	438,000
7. Kenneth Copeland	367,000
8. Dr. James Kennedy	363,000
9. "The 700 Club" (Pat Robertson)	309,000
10. "A Study in the Word" (Jimmy Swaggart)	265,000

Every evangelist among the top ten in 1985 lost audience during 1986, and Jim Bakker dropped to eleventh place with 220,000 households.

While overall audience size is much smaller than claimed (in 1980 Jerry Falwell boasted 25 million when he had no more than 1.4 million viewers), the cultural impact of the electronic church has been substantial, in part because of the political ties of many of its preachers, beginning with their support of a number of conservative causes and candidates in 1980, but also because they galvanized strong support from a relatively small group of people who for the first time found a national public articulation of their views. In effect, electronic-church programs have been the embodiment of the conservative religious revival which has been a part of every Great Awakening thus far in America.

Themes and Techniques

The electronic-church broadcasts certainly do not include *all* religious broadcasting. When we use the term here we are narrowing the field to only those TV programs which are usually 30 to 90 minutes in length, are nationally syndicated, primarily through the purchase of time, depend on a highly visible charismatic leader, exhibit high budget, "slick" production qualities, consistently solicit money over the air, and make extensive use of telephone and computerized "personalized" letter contacts with viewers. There are about two dozen such programs, and they account for the lion's share of programming time, audience viewership and audience income among the electronic-church preachers.

And what do these preachers preach? One of the most detailed studies of the electronic-church ministries was undertaken by Jeffery Hadden, a sociologist, and Charles Swann, a mainline religious broadcaster, in their book, *Primetime Preachers: The Rising Power of Televangelism.* Hadden and Swann identify three themes of the TV evangelists. First, they alleviate guilt feelings in the audience by consistent reference to the Devil: "Jesus washes away all sins and the Devil is responsible for all backsliding." Second, they emphasize the power of positive thinking: "If you would just let God be in command of your life, everything would be super A-OK. Only the Devil can mess up God's glorious plan for your life. But the Devil cannot win, if Christians would just stick together." Third, they preach that "it's all right to look out for yourself." Human selfishness, properly viewed, is not a sin.[12]

"The 700 Club," "The PTL Club," Oral Roberts, Jerry Falwell, Jimmy Swaggart and the rest of the televangelists represent the "traditionalist" religious response to the current challenge of cultural disorientation. Peter Horsfield, in his doctoral thesis on religious television, identified the themes of electronic-church programming as follows:

1. "They are authoritative at a time when authority appears to be

in disarray. The program generally centers on an authoritative, charismatic host who provides clear instruction on moral and religious problems."

2. "They place stress on the individual as the foundational societal unit, with a stress on the need for the individual to take action in the form of being born again and supporting the program. This gives the individual who is overwhelmed by the trauma he encounters in society something to do within the direction of an answer."

3. They are "generally affirmative of the social values the average American holds; reward for effort, the equal opportunity of all for success, the inherent value of (and divine imprimatur on) the American free-enterprise system." Horsfield contrasts this view of the evangelists with the mainline network programs "which often [are] critical of the American system."

4. They reinforce the belief system of the viewers "with a continual presentation of attractive and socially recognized personalities who endorse them."

5. They emphasize competition: "a battle between God and the Devil."

6. "The concrete eschatology . . . is attractive to those who see no way out of a seemingly hopeless human situation . . . . on the one hand evangelical programs proclaim the transcience and imminent end of this world, yet feature guests whose sole credential lies in their success in this world."[13]

The tactics of the electronic-church preachers in many ways are psychologically ingenious. However, in the long run many of their techniques are harmful to many viewers and listeners.

Consider, for example, a favorite electronic-church technique which might well be called the "successful people" syndrome. Almost every popular evangelical program includes interviews with persons who have made it—a singer or a well-known businessman who describes how bad things were until God was brought into the picture, but how now all is wonderful, give God the glory. The message is simple: believe in God and all will be wonderful for you, too.

There is a serious problem with this tactic. When hopeful converts begin to realize that they are not becoming especially wealthy, are not getting all the money or things they want, what can they do? Their religion prevents them from blaming God, or the preacher who claims to represent God. They can only blame *themselves,* and this pushes them deeper into self-doubt and alienation than they were originally. The "successful people" approach is bad psychology as well as bad theology.

Another favorite technique is the "give-to-get" ploy, used in one way or another by every major electronic-church evangelist. The message is: "If you give—*really* give—to God (which means to this evangelist), then God will return that gift to you and much more." The evangelists are not talking about spiritual gifts; they parade before the television screen those who have Made It Big, who asked for a car and got it, who wanted money for the down payment on a house and got it, who asked, and gave, and got.

Oral Roberts calls this the "Seed-Faith" concept. It is fundamental to his spectacular financial success. According to Jerry Scholes, who at one time was employed on Oral Roberts's senior staff, all of Roberts's books advise "You give first, and then expect miracles in your life." [14] Says Scholes, "While Seed-Faith, as a concept, indicates that you can give time, talents, or money to anyone (not necessarily Oral Roberts), the subtleties of the copy point toward giving to Oral Roberts. . . . Oral's closest associate once told me, '*Seed-Faith* put Oral's ministry back on the map.' " Roberts, "The PTL Club," "The 700 Club," and the other programs parade people across the TV screen who gave and then got something really big in return. You say you haven't gotten something back from God? Then you just haven't given enough! And so this "heavenly lottery" attracts countless thousands who even borrow money to support their evangelist and thus increase the chance of hitting it big like the folk they see on TV. But, as in any other lottery, the losers outnumber the winners a thousand to one.

"The 700 Club" has been particularly diligent in using this technique. Dick Dabney described two episodes from a "700 Club" program in 1979. Ben Kinchlow rushes up to the microphone and says to Pat Robertson:

"We have a report just in from Charlottesville, Virginia," Ben said. "A lady with an ingrown toenail sent in $100 along with her Seven Lifetime Prayer Requests. Within a week—get this—*three* of those *lifetime* prayer requests have been answered!"

"Praise *God!*" Pat said. "And that's not all," said Ben. "The toenail was miraculously healed the *very next day!*"

"Praise God!" Robertson said. "You know, you can't outgive God."
Some time later in the program, Ben once again comes on screen:

"Pat, here is a report from a woman in California," Kinchlow said, dashing up with a message just taken by one of the phone counselors. "She's on a limited income, and with all sorts of health problems, too. She decided to trust in God and to step out in faith on the Kingdom Principles. She was already giving half her disability money to The 700 Club to spread the gospel of Jesus Christ. But just last week, she decided to go *all the way,* and to give God the money she spends for cancer medicine—$120 a month. And three days later—get this!—from an entirely unexpected source, she got a check for *three thousand dollars!*"

"Praise *God! Robertson said. "Let's give God a hand!"* [15]

And permeating it all is the Madison Avenue sell. Watching Jerry Falwell's service from the Hampton Road Baptist Church one Sunday morning, I lost count after 12 sales pitches from the pulpit, for everything from lapel pins to a trip to Israel.

John Kenneth Galbraith has said that the basic purpose of advertising is to get people to buy something they don't need. Apparently, the purveyors of the electronic church think the values of the gospel are so obscure that only the hard sell can move them off the shelf. Slogans, pop songs, glad names, bad names, stacking the cards, the bandwagon—every technique basic to advertising is part of the stock-in-trade of the electronic church, which is, indeed, selling something people *don't* need—a superficial, magical God.

The electronic-church preachers, taken as a whole, represent the call for a return to "traditional" values, a call that has occurred in the early stages of each Great Awakening in America. The "traditional" values this time are a mixture of a strong and militant Americanism, a rugged individualism, anticommunism, antiintellectualism, and a return to Puritan fundamentalism.

The electronic-church message tends toward two distortions which have dogged the Christian tradition almost from its beginning. One is Manichaeism, which in the third century proposed a strong dualism that separates everything into light and darkness, spirit and matter, good and evil. The electronic-church preachers tend to pose every issue this way: either you are good or bad; America is God's while Russia is the devil's; accept Jesus and be saved or expect the hellfires of the damned on judgment day. Manichaeism was rejected by Augustine as intellectually and morally inadequate, but it has persisted in many forms throughout Christian history, and is rampant on TV religion.

A second distortion is Pelagianism, which promises considerable earthly rewards for the faithful. It denies original sin, affirms that "If I ought, I can," that all persons have the power within themselves not to sin but to do whatever they truly desire, so long as they have faith. And involved with it is the fallacy of *nominalism* ("Speak the name of the Lord Jesus Christ and you will be saved") which fits nicely into the electronic church's emphasis on the individual. This particularly American distortion was popularized in the 1950s by Norman Vincent Peale, and more recently by this spiritual descendant, Robert Schuller, though it is a hallmark of all the electronic-church preachers.

One of the great appeals of the electronic-church gospel is that it gives religious sanction to the American tradition of utilitarian self-interest. Robert Bellah has shown that American culture from its early beginnings has held two views in tension: on the one hand, the biblical understanding of community based on the notion of charity for all members, a community supported by public and private virtue; and, on the other hand, the utilitarian understanding that community is a neutral state which allows individuals to pursue the maximization of their self-interest.[16] The electronic church harmonizes these conflicting traditions by corrupting the biblical tradition so that religion itself becomes the key to maximizing self-interest, and there is no effective linkage to virtue, charity, or community. This corruption of the fundamental biblical concept of *conscience* into *self-interest* is perhaps the most serious of all the electronic church's distortions.

It is here that the insidious and pernicious effect of the technological era and The Technique becomes clear. The Technique takes as its key value *what works*. Applied to the electronic church, whose basic objective is to "win people to Christ," whatever technology, whatever selling techniques, whatever psychological ploys and gambits that are "effective" in getting more income and more stations and more audience are good, simply because they *work*.

Also, whatever maximizes self-interest works. And the programs do both. This explains why the electronic church is phenomenally successful in fund-raising and growth, because it is technologically sophisticated in the ways of this world, and because its message is finally one of self-interest. It also explains why it fails to meet the minimum requirements of biblical Christianity, because ultimately it places technique above substance, means above ends, things above people, and people against people.

Finances and Power

Fund-raising is a central activity, if not *the* central activity, of the electronic church. A number of ethical issues center around the methods employed in fund-raising, the lack of accountability in the use of the money, and the high costs of promotion and administration in relation to the amounts actually going for the projects and causes for which the funds were raised.

The amounts of money are not small. Income for CBN in 1983 totaled $230 million; for Jerry Falwell's "Gospel Hour," Liberty University, and Thomas Road Baptist Church, donations were $53 million in 1985; Jim and Tammy Bakker's PTL took in $72.1 million in 1985 from contributions, real estate sales, lodging, food, and retail sales, and the sale of time on his cable network.[17]

In general, appeals for money dominate the programs of electronic evangelism. Robert Abelman, professor of communications at Cleveland State University, in a study of the content of 40 leading religious shows in 1983, discovered that during an average hour, a televangelist asked each viewer to donate $328. The person who watches two hours a week is subjected to direct appeals for a total of $31,500 a year. "Most often, the reason cited for the request for money is survival," Abelman reported. "It's not to preach the Gospel or for mission work. It's to stay on the air."[18]

CBN in many ways is the most active and sophisticated of the big operators. Callers to CBN's telephone prayer counseling centers are asked, first, whether they know Jesus Christ and, second, whether they would like to be a member of "The 700 Club." There are several levels of membership. CBN supporters can join The 1000 Club by paying $1000 a year, or The 2500 Club at $2500 a year, and those who contribute $5000 or more a year become members of The Founders' Club. Robertson claimed in 1985 that the overall operations of CBN took in $230 million, "give or take $30 million." The Internal Revenue Service records show revenue in 1983 for CBN—excluding the for-profit TV-cable network and other enterprises—was $101 million, of which $89 million came as donations. That same year CBN gave a total of $6.9 million in gifts to CBN University and other mission ministries, or less than 8% of total income.[19]

Following a storm of criticism about the lack of financial accountability on the part of many of the TV evangelists, the groups in the early 1970s established the Evangelical Council for Financial Accountability to develop financial accounting and reporting principles to which all members must adhere—a kind of Good Housekeeping Seal of Approval. CBN is not a member of the council, and it does not meet the Council of Better Business Bureaus standards for organizations that solicit charitable contributions.

In 1978 the State of Massachusetts sued CBN for failing to disclose its finances in accordance with state law. CBN reorganized, created a for-profit arm called CBN Continental Broadcasting Inc., and the suit was dropped. But Kevin Suffern, an assistant attorney general for Massachusetts, said, "If you are dealing with millions and millions of dollars and you set up a system of corporations and subcorporations and for-profit and not-for-profit arms, and you do not have an overall requirement of financial disclosure, you are never going to be able to trace all that money."[20]

The Falwell organization also does not subscribe to the Evangelical Council for Financial Responsibility, and it does not comply with the Better Business Bureau standards for charitable organizations that solicit funds. In 1979, income raised by Falwell's television program was $35 million, while its operating costs for direct-mail appeals, promotion, and administration—including maintaining Falwell's 12-room house and his private Westwind II jet—amounted to $26 million. And there were some disquieting differences between what Falwell said was happening and what was actually going on. For instance, in 1980 Falwell refused to pay $67,000 in taxes on land which was not tax-exempt. One of the officers of "The Old-Time Gospel Hour" told reporters at the time that the church owned no property not "involved in the ministry of the gospel of Jesus Christ," when in fact it was leasing space to a supermarket, a gift shop, and a restaurant-bar in the shopping plaza which contained its offices.[21]

Jim Bakker of "The PTL Club" has consistently spent more than he has taken in. For example, income for 1985 was $72.1 million, with $42 million of that coming from direct contributions and the rest earned from a new $30 million Victorian-style hotel, a motel, restaurant and other activities associated with his biblical-theme amusement park, the 2500-acre Heritage USA. PTL's expenses that same year were $89.7 million. The ministry showed a deficit of $17.5 million.[22]

Also, Bakker has been accused a number of times of diverting money collected for mission projects to pay ongoing expenses. In the late 1970s Bakker made several tearful on-air pleas for money, saying that he and his wife Tammy had given "every penny of our life savings to PTL." A month later, Bakker made a $6000 down payment on a house-boat. In addition to his waterfront parsonage near Charlotte, North Carolina, Bakker owns a second house in Palm Desert, California, a Rolls Royce, and a Mercedes-Benz.[23]

The Federal Communications Commission has investigated charges of PTL diverting funds raised on the air. Instead of ruling on the purported misuse of funds, however, the FCC approved PTL's immediate sale of its television station in Canton, Ohio, which ended the Commission's official jurisdiction over PTL. Three of the seven FCC commissioners voted against the action, saying they dissented "from its stench." Commissioners Joseph R. Fogarty and Henry M. Rivera wrote that PTL was "under a cloud of serious misconduct, including substantial and material questions of fradulent duty, false testimony."[24]

The reported income for Jimmy Swaggart in 1982 was about $45 million. Swaggart was on 223 TV stations in the United States and claimed to have about one million persons on his mailing list. Two-thirds of those who contribute to Swaggart send in less than $10 per month; the average giving is about $45 per person a year.

A 1983 study in central Ohio, situated in the Bible Belt, showed that about two-thirds of all households there contributed to local church-es, while about 15% contribute to electronic preachers. Swaggart was the highest-rated evangelist in central Ohio, even though he reached only about 2% of all the households.

Swaggart says that about 95% of his support comes from church-goers. Of his $45 million income in 1982, he spent about $38 million—more than 80%—just keeping his program on the air, that is, on pro-duction and distribution. For every two dollars he spent on production he spent another dollar buying television time. However, thanks to his TV income, Swaggart says he is able to feed 20,000 children a day in poor parts of the world and to build churches in those areas. He regularly appears on 200 stations *outside* the United States.[25]

Most of the major televangelists' income and expenses fit this general pattern. Frances FitzGerald, in an extensive *New Yorker* article in 1982, showed that Jerry Falwell spent $5 in fund-raising for every $7 he raised—a high ratio indeed (71.4%).[26] By way of contrast, the Rev. Norman Dewire, the chief program coordinating executive for the United Methodist Church, points out that "the national United Methodist Church runs on five cents of each $1, supports 750 missionaries, 900 short-term missionaries, curriculum and worship materials, the largest network of private colleges in the United States, one hundred retirement homes, and the recruitment and training of ministers plus all communication materials."[27]

The prodigious cost of promotion versus results among the electronic-church ministries is even greater than average in the case of "The PTL Club." In his study on the televangelists, Peter Horsfield did some interesting arithmetic with Jim Bakker's claim that, due to "The PTL" program, 28,143 people received Christ as Savior in 1979 and that "these new converts would represent a new church of over 500 people every week started by PTL."[28] But, Horsfield points out, 80% of those respondents are already either associated with a church or soon drop out, leaving 20% *at most* who might join a church. This works out to a *possible* new church of 500 created once a month rather than once a week. Given an annual expenditure of $50 million, the cost of establishing these 12 new churches a year would average $7.9 million per church, or $9,345 per convert![29]

In March 1987, Jim Bakker suddenly resigned as head of PTL, asserting that six years earlier he had engaged in a sexual encounter with a church secretary, that he had "succumbed to blackmail" about the incident as part of a "diabolical plot" to take over PTL, and that he was resigning in order to prevent a "hostile takeover" by a "well-known individual."[30] However, shortly before Bakker's resignation, his denomination, the Assemblies of God, had revealed that it was conducting a formal investigation into allegations of Bakker's sexual misconduct.

Bakker's lawyer accused Jimmy Swaggart of trying to take over PTL. Swaggart denied the accusation, saying, "I don't know what I would do with PTL if I had it," but he readily admitted to having taken the matter of Bakker's improprieties to the leadership of the Assemblies of God, to which Swaggart also belongs. Swaggart was harshly critical of Bakker, saying that "the entire debacle" was "a cancer that needed to be excised from the body of Christ."[31] And Pat Robertson, whose 700 Club was where Bakker got his start, said of the incident, "I think the Lord is housecleaning a little bit. I'm glad to see it happen." But Oral Roberts, who earlier in the year had drawn considerable criticism himself by announcing that God had told him that, unless he raised $8 million by March 31, he would be "called home," supported Bakker and criticized Swaggart for "sowing discord among the brethren."[32]

A week after Bakker's resignation statement, the Rev. G. Raymond Carlson, general superintendent of the Assemblies of God, said, "We do not find there is any evidence of blackmail. To the contrary, the evidence seems to indicate that effort and money have been expended to cover moral failure."[33]

Bakker turned over the leadership of PTL to Jerry Falwell, who immediately set out to reduce the friction which had developed between the top evangelists and which the press had gleefully dubbed "the Holy War." Speaking generally about the sharp exchanges between the TV evangelists, Dr. Carl C. F. Henry, a long-time observer of the electronic church, said, "There's a great deal of ambition. It's very expensive to run those television stations, and if you fall behind in your fund-raising for a single week it can be devastating. So there is a lot of competition."[34]

There is nothing unusual about making money, especially in America. But it certainly has been unusual for religious evangelists, until now. Jonathan Edwards, the great 18th-century revivalist, lived all his life on a pastor's salary. Charles G. Finney, the spectacular revivalist of the mid-1800s, received a modest salary as evangelist and later as a college president. Dwight L. Moody lived completely on faith and took no salary after he became an evangelist in the late 1800s. Before this generation, only Billy Sunday's crusades made substantial sums, and Sunday himself was worth only $50,000 when he died. Even Billy Graham has always taken a modest salary from the Billy Graham Evangelist Association and made certain that he did not control the use of the association's funds single-handedly.

For today's electronic evangelists the situation is quite different. Most of them have truly enormous organizations working for them— often hundreds of men and women whose livelihoods depend upon one man. They have built large institutions—Oral Roberts University, the

City of Faith, the Crystal Cathedral, the CBN University, Liberty College. And while their salaries are usually in the range of middle managers in the business world, they also command formidable goods and services: jet airplanes for their personal use, automobiles, homes and vacation retreats, a staff devoted strictly to their travel and comfort needs, bodyguards, public relations offices, unlimited expense accounts—the kind of perquisites only top leaders in business or government can command. In addition, they receive huge amounts of donations which are entirely undesignated—which, in effect, can be used by them for whatever they wish. Their organizations are incorporated, of course, but usually the Board of Directors is a closely knit family affair, with the evangelist, his wife, their sons or daughters as the members. The fact is that each televangelist possesses truly enormous economic power.

With the economic power comes social and political power. It is no accident that Oral Roberts is on the board of several of the largest banks in Tulsa; after all, the university and 60-story-hospital are big business. But even Oral Roberts's political dreams have been paltry in comparison with two of his fellow televangelists: Jerry Falwell and Pat Robertson.

Politics

Historically, most fundamentalists have preached withdrawal from the world as the only way to remain untainted by sin. The power plays and compromises of politics were something clearly for Christians to avoid. As late as 1976 Jerry Falwell said in an interview in *Playboy* that his criticisms of Jimmy Carter were "those of a pastor speaking on a moral issue" and were not intended to be political.

But in the late 1970s Paul Weyrich, a founder of the Moral Majority, realized the new movement had to have a prominent and telegenic minister to lead the movement, and he chose Jerry Falwell. Falwell immediately was catapulted from being pastor of one of the country's fastest-growing churches (the 20,000 member Thomas Road Baptist Church) to being the national spear-carrier for the extreme political right. Since then, many other evangelists, notably Rex Humbard, Jimmy Swaggart, Jim Bakker, and James Robison, have joined in politicizing their religion on the airwaves.

Falwell energetically used the press and the popular media to spread his political gospel. He told his television audience to fight against pornography, abortion, homosexuality, secular humanism, and promiscuity. He urged them to stand up for morality, patriotism, school prayer, and a strong national defense. He called the National Organization of Women the "National Order of Witches." When a reporter questioned him about his calling for the killing of Libyan leader Muammar Qaddafi, he replied, with a smile, "I'm a Baptist, not a Quaker." He called Nobel peace-prize winner Archbishop Desmond Tutu of South Africa "a phony." [35]

Polsters regularly report that most people view Falwell unfavorably. But his followers support him with an enthusiasm bordering on fanaticism. They see his unpopularity as the result of his outspoken leadership, plus the bias and distortion of the mass media.

The Republican party refused to credit Falwell's Moral Majority with a decisive role in the 1980 election, and Falwell and his followers have made a difference in only a few very close elections, such as the 1984 U.S. Senate race in North Carolina between then Governor Jim Hunt, a Democrat, and incumbent Republican Jesse Helms; Helms won with 51.3% of the vote. On the other hand, many Virginia and national Democrats believe that the controversy surrounding Falwell cancels any help he brings to the Republican Party. Since Falwell began supporting Republicans in Virginia, Democrats have won the state's top offices twice and recaptured the congressional district that includes Lynchburg, Falwell's home town, when that district formerly had been Republican for three decades.

As to the inconsistent political stance of Falwell in 1980, Frances FitzGerald points out that Falwell represents a bridging of southern pietistic withdrawal from society with the economic success story of the New South. "While Thomas Road people want separation, authority, and certainty, they also want career advancement, some worldly goods, and a little power in the society. The conflicting aims go a long way toward explaining the confusion of fundamentalists' politics in the 1980 election."

On one hand, Falwell was saying that "the [local] church should be a disciplined charging army. . . . Christians, like slaves and soldiers, ask no questions." But when he went forth to do battle with the world outside Lynchburg, Virginia, he discovered that the old rhetoric would not work. The reporters demanded consistency. The Republican leadership was "asking him to look like a tolerant, conservative sort of fellow." Thus Falwell had to develop a different public from the one he was used to, and this public did not go away when Falwell jetted back to the Thomas Road Baptist Church, as he did almost every Sunday, to preach in his old tone of voice to his old audience.[36]

But if Jerry Falwell is an advance guard of political conservatism, Pat Robertson is a master strategist. Robertson lets Falwell act as his lightning rod. If the sparks fly when Falwell takes a position, Robertson backs off; if the going is relatively smooth, then Robertson says the same thing Falwell says—but six months later.

Robertson, the son of a former U.S. senator, has far more money than Falwell, a much larger TV audience, and considerably more political savvy. He has always done things in a big way. By his own account, he started with a bank balance of $3 and built a $230 million empire that supports a university, a library, and social work and mission organizations. He also takes credit publicly for turning Hurricane Gloria away from Virginia Beach in October 1985. Says Robertson, "When you pray to command a hurricane to go out into the Atlantic Ocean, it isn't like saying, 'The Lord bless you.' "[37]

Robertson appears to have presidential aspirations. Any other job, he told an interviewer, would be a *lateral* move. During a press conference in 1986 following a $2500-per-couple fund-raising dinner in Washington, Robertson said to reporters, "It's electric. There are tens of thousands of people who are on their feet cheering. They are saying, 'Go for it. We want you' . . . . And I'm listening."[38] Whether or not he is successful in reaching the White House in 1988, by then Robertson will be only 58, and there will always be 1992 . . . and 1996. "We have enough votes to run the country," he was quoted as saying at the "Washington for Jesus" rally in 1980. "And when the people say, 'We've had enough,' we are going to take over."[39]

Thus far we have been discussing the electronic church from the point of view of the evangelists themselves, the tradition out of which they have come, their use of radio and television technology, their message and techniques.

But what about the listeners and viewers? Who are they, why do they tune in, and what effect is the electronic church having on them?

SIX

THE ELECTRONIC CHURCH AND ITS AUDIENCE

Lord, when did we see thee hungry and feed thee, or
thirsty and give thee drink?

(Matt. 25:37)

Who Is Watching, and Why?

In 1980, I was asked by *TV Guide* to write an article on the electronic
church. The piece was published in mid-July with the cover headline
"Why TV Evangelists Can't Be Pastors." In the article I listed some
of the innovations of the electronic evangelists, and then raised five
questions:

● Does the electronic church separate people from their own community?

● Is the electronic church good evangelism?

● Has the electronic church become captive to commercial broadcasting?

● Are the values implicit in most successful electronic church programs actually the values of the secular society it pretends to reject?

● Is the electronic church driving religious diversity off the air?

In a summary paragraph I said that the electronic church helps some
people but misleads far more, and that in the long run it probably is
doing more harm than good.

I had expected to get letters in rebuttal, since *TV Guide* reaches some
47 million readers. But I was not prepared for the deluge of letters
that came in, almost 500 in all. Most, though not all, were supportive

of the electronic evangelists. I replied to every letter that could be answered.

The letters were so intriguing and informative that I kept a tally of their basic points. Two-thirds of the writers were women, ranging in age from 15 to 90, and several correspondents made a point of saying that they were "not a frumpy old lady" or "not middle rural America." There was one "Truck Driver for Jesus" and one Jesuit Ph.D., but most merely described themselves in one way or another as born-again Christians.

Four basic themes emerged from the critical group. One, quite predictably, was a strong defense of various electronic-church programs. For example, "I, for one, have found a *personal* relationship with Jesus Christ by watching the 700 Club and PTL Club." And, "Personally, Oral Roberts has made my day many times when I was depressed, and he does write me back."

A second response, almost as predictable, was a litany of the ills of our nation, focusing primarily on homosexuality, abortion, anti-Christian TV programs, and communism.

A third theme, often linked with the second, was the view that the solution to the problems facing America is to establish a theocracy. A fairly typical letter proclaimed, "I believe that the USA was founded as a Nation Under God and has had God's grace all these years and only when the laws and Supreme Court decisions started to give more power to the secular groups has God's Grace begun to diminish and soon we will no longer be a blessed nation."

But the theme I was not prepared for, either as to its intensity or its pervasiveness, was an angry outpouring against local churches and their preachers. Letter after letter accused the local church of being dry, unfriendly, cold, not filled with the Spirit, unbiblical, works of Satan, dead, or dying. "So many of the Starched Collar Ministers [these writers loved capital letters] don't bother to help others after they preach their sermon and shake hands. It's a cold howdy-do and goodbye." Or, "when I needed Christ I got social and community planning and programs and softball but no Jesus. People want truth and salvation." And, "PTL is better than any church I have ever attended, which is quite a few." Finally: "The (so-called) electronic church has done a more valuable service to this country as well as many others than any boring, unholy-ghost-filled church around."

A few writers defended their local church, indicating that they attended regularly while also listening—usually daily—to the electronic preachers. But by and large the responses indicated that the local church simply is not meeting the needs of many, many people.

Unfortunately, the perception of many mainline churches as dry, unfriendly, and moribund is not just a religious problem, for the vacuum that is created has spawned a crisis in the society as a whole. Franklin Littell points out that totalitarian creeds and systems have always arisen and come to power at times and places where religion was tired, ineffective, corrupted by privilege, and lacking in appeal to youth. From what I could determine from the letters, a goodly number of those who took up their pens to defend the electronic church against my criticisms are ready and waiting for some kind of totalitarian solution.

Many are lonely. Many are sick and tired of what life has dealt them. They want a part of the American dream: "The Bible says we are called to be the head not the tail and should have the best. . . . Please answer this as soon as possible and write back to me."

Some sought solutions in prejudice: "It's the Jews like Mike Wallace that keep on persecuting Christians and they are in a position to be heard."

Some already are in thrall to authority: "I go to my own church three times a week. But whenever possible I do listen to Bro. Falwell. I am sure he doesn't want me to do otherwise."

A few are consumed by hatred: "P.S. Keep your hands off the work of God. You have no right!" And from an anonymous cassette tape recording: "Doctor William F. Fore—it will give me great pleasure to slit your throat!"

Reading and answering these letters brought me to the disturbing conclusion that while the electronic-church programs may be providing inadequate and even misleading and harmful solutions to the needs of many of their listeners and viewers, at least they are bringing to the American scene an accurate awareness of what those needs are. And if my correspondents are reasonably representative of the electronic-church audience, most of the mainline churches are *not even aware* of the nature or the depth of the needs of these millions of men and women who live within reach of their own buildings and services and congregations.

What are their needs? They are simple: to be recognized, to be needed, to be of worth, to live in a world that can be understood, to be secure. And the issues that bother them are the very ones that bother members of the mainline churches: war and peace, the misuse of sex, the unjust use of political and economic power, how to find useful work and satisfying play, how to maintain a society open to many points of view, how to have relationships with other persons that are meaningful and rewarding.

These letters drove home to me the sobering fact that the electronic church *is* a formidable threat to mainline churches today, not because it threatens to reduce income or attendance, but because it has revealed a critical failure on the part of most mainline churches to deal with many of the people in their own neighborhoods. To their everlasting shame, the mainline churches have simply failed to understand and meet the needs of a significant number of people in their communities, people who are searching for a satisfying religious experience, but who have not found it in the mainline churches. These people, many of them alienated, unfulfilled, forgotten, or ignored, but also many dynamic, independent, and searching, are going to find what solace and direction they can from the superficial and ultimately harmful ministrations of the electronic church, if they cannot find it in the mainline churches. For all of its problems, the electronic church at least has not *ignored* them.

Research Results

Debate over the effectiveness of the new television ministries raged between the mainline churches and the electronic-church groups throughout the 1970s. Was the electronic church luring members away from the local church, or was it encouraging members to attend more regularly? Was it taking money from local churches or was it furthering overall giving? Was it an effective new evangelistic tool or was it merely reaching the already committed?

Mainline church leaders as well as many evangelical leaders tended to be critical of the electronic church. Its supporters were euphoric about its, and their, new-found power and prestige. However, neither side was able to buttress arguments with solid facts, because very little research had been focused directly on the new phenomenon. The charges and countercharges became all the more strident because of the lack of real information.

In July 1980 the National Council of Churches' Communication Commission and the National Religious Broadcasters jointly issued an invitation to key groups on both sides of the controversy to join in a major research project to get at the facts. As a result the Ad Hoc Committee on Religious Television Research was formed, surely one of the century's most broadly based religious coalitions. Eventually the $175,000 project was funded by some 39 groups—ranging from "The Old-Time Gospel Hour" (Jerry Falwell) and the Christian Broadcasting Network (Pat Robertson) to the U.S. Catholic Conference, the Episcopal Church and the United Church of Christ, and with representation from virtually every part of the religious spectrum in between.

The controlling idea was that even though each side disagreed with the other as to tactic and strategy, both wanted solid information. The groups could strive to agree on what questions they both wanted answered, and once the questions were clear, they could cooperate to hire the best professional researchers to find the answers. A significant advantage of this approach was that neither side could later attempt to discredit the results of the research on the basis that "they asked the wrong questions."

The Annenberg School of Communications at the University of Pennsylvania was hired as the primary contractor, with the Gallup Organization of Princeton, New Jersey, conducting the national survey. After two years of planning, field work, and analysis, the results were announced at a press conference held at the Graduate Center of New York City University on April 16, 1984.[1]

The study, consisting of two volumes and buttressed by dozens of charts, made the following major points:

1. *The viewing audience for the electronic church programs is far smaller than had been claimed.* In 1982 a Gallup survey found that 43% of the total population said that they had watched religious programming in the past 30 days, and another Gallup poll in 1981 showed that 32% said that they had watched during the past week. This would work out to some 71 million viewers per week.

But what people *claim* and what they *do* are very different. Researchers have long known that people have a tendency to say what they think would please those asking the questions. For example, years ago public broadcasters discovered, to their sorrow, that the people who said they wanted more symphonies and ballet on TV really preferred to watch movies. To get around this problem with religious-TV viewers, the Annenberg researchers went to several previous months of Arbitron television viewers' diaries, looked up the actual programs watched by day, hour, and channel in the *TV Guide,* and thereby identified "confirmed viewing"—in other words, what people *really* watched.

This information told a far different story. According to the diaries, there is a total *duplicated* national religious television audience of 24.7 million weekly for religious television programs. But this number includes many of the same people counted two, three, or even a dozen times—if they watched that many programs during a week. Taking into account that the diaries may underreport by as much as 15%, the study estimated that an unduplicated audience of 13.3 million people watched at least 15 minutes of religious TV per week. This amounts to 6.2% of the national TV audience.

Unfortunately, this key finding was based on a questionable assumption. What Arbitron really provided was only the number of *households* viewing, and the households were then multiplied by the number of people assumed to be watching, to give the total audience. Annenberg researchers assumed 2.4 persons, which is the national average number of persons per household. But almost all religious programming is scheduled during fringe or even deep-fringe time, when the figure of 1.4 persons per household is usually used by the broadcasting industry. If this 1.4 figure is used, the number of people watching 15 minutes or more per week is 7.2 million.

But this is the number of people who watch only *15 minutes per week* or more, and 15 minutes per week is not very much when the average viewer spends more than 30 hours per week watching TV. If we take the number of people who tune in *one hour* or more per week— a more realistic definition of the "regular" viewer—the figures are considerably smaller, and, using the 1.4 person-per-household estimate, there are about *3.76 million persons, or approximately 1.69% of the total population, who watch one hour or more of religious TV each week.*

Two years after the Annenberg-Gallup study was released, Pat Robertson's CBN commissioned the A. C. Nielsen Company to measure the electronic-church viewing audience again, including, for the first time, the cable-TV viewers, since CBN is carried on thousands of cable systems. CBN itself released the information from the proprietary study, amid considerable fanfare, reporting that the top ten religious programs attracted 40.2% or 61 million American households during February 1984.[2]

However, analysis by Stewart M. Hoover of the original Annenberg research team revealed that this information was misleading.[3] The data measured anyone who had watched at least *six minutes* of any one of the programs during the whole month of February. Also, it measured the percent of viewers who were viewing at the time the top-ten programs were on the air—periods such as early Sunday mornings when the total number of viewers is very small. The 40.2% turned out to be a percentage of only 33 million viewers, in contrast to the more than 100 million persons who view during prime time each evening. Hoover also pointed out that any program has a certain probability of being selected at random, and that a program on the air when there are few viewers has a greater chance of being selected completely at random.

He concluded that it is unlikely that the overall, unduplicated *weekly* audience for these programs is any larger than the 13.3 million originally estimated by the Annenberg study. He also showed from the Nielsen statistics that those who subscribe to cable TV are actually *less* likely to view religious programs than those without cable.[4]

2. *The electronic church is not effective evangelism, although it is an effective reinforcer of the existing religious beliefs of viewers.* The Annenberg study reported: "The audience for religious programs on television is not an essentially new, or young, or varied audience. Viewers of religious programs are by and large also the believers, the church-goers, the contributors. Their viewing . . . appears to be an expression, a confirmation of a set of religious beliefs and not a substitute for them."[5]

The research gave us a helpful profile of the average viewers. They are somewhat older, lower in education and income, more conservative, more "fundamentalist" and more likely to live in rural areas of the South and Midwest than are nonviewers. Heavy viewers (those who watch one hour or more per week) are largely Southern Baptist (19%) and other Baptists (21%), followed by charismatic Christians (10.5%), Catholics (10%), United Methodists (8.3%) and other Methodists (7.1%). The rest of the mainline churches, such as Presbyterian, Lutheran, Disciples, United Church of Christ, and Episcopalian, each make up less than 2% of the viewing audience.

Fully 77% of the heavy viewers of religious TV are church members, and almost all of them attend church at least once a month. Regardless of their denominational affiliation, they are much more likely than nonviewers to read the Bible, to pray frequently, to take the Bible literally, to believe "that Jesus Christ will return to earth someday," to report having been "born again," to believe in miracles, and to favor "speaking in tongues." They thus scored high on what the researchers called their "literalist/charismatic" scale.

When heavy viewers were asked whether watching religious television had changed their involvement in the local church, 7% said it had increased, and 3% said it had decreased their involvement. One in six said that religious TV contributed more than their church to their spiritual life, and one in three said that it contributed more than their church to their information about moral and social issues.

Fourteen percent said that their viewing of religious programs was "a substitute for going to church," and about 20% said that they watched religious programs on Sundays during church hours. Of course, this figure includes many of the ill, the elderly, and those who could not readily go out to church, regardless of whether the electronic-church programs were on the air.

The Gallup summary pointed out that while religious-TV viewing does not seem to be associated with lower levels of church attendance, volunteer work, or church contributions among the heavy viewers taken as a whole, it does seem to be associated with *lower* religious involvement among persons over 50, divorced persons, those who require assistance in going places, persons with low levels of education, and those who have become dissatisfied with their local church. In other words, while the electronic church probably is not causing much of a decrease in mainline church attendance, it does provide an attractive alternative for a relatively small group who find watching television an acceptable substitute for attending church.

Financial giving to the cause of their choice is another way people reinforce their religious beliefs. The most highly visible electronic-church ministries were the most likely to request money, and their requests were numerous—40% of all programs included at least three requests for money during the course of each telecast. The average requested ranged from a minimum of $31 and up to $600 per program. No mainline program in the survey asked for a specific amount of money.

Most people who gave to the electronic church also gave to their local church, and vice versa. However, only 6% of all viewers were regular contributors to religious programs. An additional 13% contributed "once in a while," and 5% more gave to "special appeals only." But those who did give, gave a great deal. Of the 6% regular contributors, 40% gave to three or more programs. Their contributions averaged $35.17 *per contribution,* and the mean *total* contribution was $95.24 per year.

Another part of the reinforcing process is individual contact. One-third of viewers said that they had been contacted by mail during the past year. Twenty percent said they had received five or more letters, and 11% reported that they had written to or called the programs they watched. On the other hand, only 3% said that they had received a telephone call from any of the programs.

One of the more revealing questions had to do with "outreach" by the viewers themselves. Viewers were asked with whom they often discussed the programs they watched. The replies were: family (23%), friends (13%), and others at church (6%). Only 5% mentioned that they ever discussed the programs with their pastors.

Heavy viewers watch broadcasts which affirm what they already believe. The national survey used the "literalist/charismatic" index of evangelical belief (as opposed to membership in an evangelical denomination), which showed that holding these beliefs was more strongly associated with the viewing of religious programs than *any* other single factor—including attending church, contributing to a church, participating in community activities, income, age, or sex. *Belief* in the "literalist/charismatic" worldview was the most important single factor in determining whether a person watched religious television.

The conclusion drawn from the research is that electronic-church broadcasts rarely speak to people outside their natural constituency, but speak to people already highly "religious" in terms of their literalistic and charismatic beliefs. Electronic-church programs, in the words of the researchers, "serve primarily to express and cultivate, rather than extend or broaden, existing religious beliefs in the lives of viewers who turn to them."

3. *The roles of people are essentially the same in the symbolic worlds of both the electronic-church programs and general television programs.* We have seen the way in which television cultivates a worldview

by defining "roles" which people play—telling who is important, who is not, which people can do what. The researchers found that the roles that people play in the world of *religious* TV are by and large the same as the roles they play in *general* TV.

In the programming of both religious and general TV, men outnumber women three to one. In both, men are dominant. In both, women tend to be young. In both, the professions are vastly overrepresented, although the clergy are very prominent in religious TV while they hardly appear at all in general commercial programs. Perhaps most important, as the study puts it, "in both prime-time drama and religious programs, blue-collar workers, the unemployed, the retired and housewives are practically invisible."[6]

The worlds of religious TV and general TV are also similar with regard to children and the elderly. While children and adolescents comprise about a third of the U.S. population, they account for only 4% on religious TV and 6% on general TV. The elderly, about 12% of our population, make up little more than 3% of those appearing on either religious or general programs. Nonwhites are also underrepresented in relation to their real numbers in the actual population.

However, religious TV contains a few unique distortions all its own. Five per cent of all participants in religious programs claim to have been healed either during or after the telecasts, and the healers on the programs play major roles. But most recipients of healing are women, and healers are men. It is men who are the clergy, who quote the Bible (and its authority), and men do not suffer from as many ailments or personal problems as do women.

The world of religious TV has even more ailments and personal problems than general TV. Fully three-quarters of the programs mention family, financial and health problems, unemployment, or physical handicaps. The solutions are usually "spiritual" in nature. The researchers were able to identify only one specific cure proposed for all ailments, namely, making a financial contribution to the program. In fact, financial contribution as a solution was suggested on one-fourth of all the prominent electronic-church ministries. It was never mentioned on mainline church programs.

4. *For most heavy viewers of religious television, watching the programs is both an expression of belief and an act of protest against the world of general television.*

Dean George Gerbner and his Annenberg School team have been studying American television for more than 20 years. One of their most significant findings is that general television has a "mainstream" effect in our culture. That is, TV cultivates a commonality of outlook that tends to be shared by *all* heavy viewers. We have seen that general television is, in many ways, the common mass ritual of American civil religion. Therefore we should not be surprised at their finding that general television relates to and cultivates religiosity in its own way. The Annenberg report boldly suggests that "commercial television viewing may supply or supplant (or both) some religious satisfactions and thus lessen the importance of religion for its heavy viewers."[7]

But in its study of religious television, the Annenberg team also discovered something new. They found that there are *two* television mainstreams, and the two differ greatly from each other. *Religious* TV's mainstream tends to be conservative and restrictive and puritanical. *General* TV's mainstream tends to be politically moderate, somewhat restrictive, and populist but not puritanical.

This means there are significant differences in the attitudes and values of the viewers of each mainstream. Heavy viewers of religious television are more likely than light viewers to describe themselves as conservative, to oppose a nuclear freeze, and to favor tougher laws against pornography. They also are much more likely to have voted in the last election, which helps identify one of the strengths of the electronic-church movement.

Heavy viewers of general television tend to describe themselves as politically moderate, are more likely than light viewers to favor a nuclear freeze, and are not as concerned with pornography. They are far *less* likely to have voted in the last election than light viewers, which goes a long way toward explaining the continuing reduction in the percentage of those who vote in general elections in the United States.

Heavy viewers of religious TV tend to attend church, but heavy viewers of general TV tend *not* to attend church. The same difference in response holds true for making contributions to the local church, for participating in nonworship activities at a church, and for social attitudes such as upholding the traditional role of women, being dissatisfied with today's moral climate and holding traditional and more restrictive sexual values.

Religious conservatives sense this conflict between the worldview of general television and their own worldview. For this reason they understand their viewing of *religious* programs as both an act of protest against the "evils" of general television and an affirmation of their support for the worldview expressed within the electronic-church programs.

These characteristics of the mainstream of general television are significant, because for many years general television has been functioning as a powerful, if not the most powerful, cultivator of our society's overall values, attitudes, and behavior. It may well be, as the study puts it, that "for matters of religious importance, experience, participation and dollars, the churches' principal competition is not the television ministry but general television."[8]

Research Implications

What conclusions can we draw from the research findings? First, while the electronic church does not represent a serious institutional threat to the mainline churches, it does pose a threat to mainline theology, particularly in the areas of mission, evangelism, and education. The electronic church is not an institutional threat, because its audience is relatively small and static. Two-thirds of its viewers are not affiliated with mainline churches, and those who are by and large are giving both to their local church and to the television ministries of their choice. Furthermore, more than three-fourths are members of some church, and attend regularly.

But the research shows that the electronic-church programs consolidate and reinforce a restrictive and narrow view both of religion and of the world. Evangelism, in the sense of reaching out to find and convert people not already reached, is ineffective, although in some of the ministries much is made of the importance of reaching people *outside* the United States. Mission is focused on nurturing those who already strongly hold literalist/charismatic beliefs. Education is essentially one-way, emphasizing the obligation to make financial contributions to keep the program going. Furthermore, most of the distortions of general television are found within religious television, except that sexism, authoritarianism, and an emphasis on simple and crass answers to problems are even more blatant. At almost every point, the underlying theology of the electronic church is at odds with the theologies of the mainline churches.

At the press conference announcing the Annenberg-Gallup study, a member of the audience, himself an electronic-church broadcaster, summed up the report by stating, rather wistfully, "It looks like the research is saying that all that religious TV is doing is to make people feel good and to get them to keep on doing what they're doing!"—to which one of the researchers replied: "That's exactly right!"

Second, the research revealed that it is *general television,* not religious television, that is really challenging people's belief systems and their church attendance and financial support. It is the heavy viewers of general TV who attend the least, give the least, and believe the least. And, of course, general TV is far more pervasive than religious TV.

It is clear from the research that a major task confronting religious organizations must be to learn how to deal with television, so that people can control it rather than be controlled by it. Unfortunately, the research also shows that the electronic church, by adopting the utilitarian "whatever works is good" approach of The Technique, has become part of the problem rather than part of the solution. However, both the electronic church and the mainline churches are dwarfed by the immensity of the challenges posed by the power of television itself.

Electronic Church in the Balance

If we take into account the analysis of the message of the electronic church, and the findings of the research, how, on balance, does the electronic church come out? I identify two positive contributions made by the electronic church, and five negative consequences.

First, the electronic church has developed an extremely accurate diagnosis of the spiritual hunger of millions of people who are reacting intuitively against the inhuman and unchristian worldview of our media culture. The TV evangelists understand that people are hurting because they feel ignored and not needed, because they are often treated like commodities by business and like dummies by politicians, because they doubt their own worth and feel they have no real say in how their world is run.

The motion picture "Network" contains a memorable scene that describes the way such people feel today. In that film, the TV newscaster, like the electronic-church preachers, discovered that there is a vast group out there who are alienated and deeply frustrated. On his newscast he tells them to go to the nearest window, throw it open and shout to the world, "I'm as mad as Hell, and I'm not going to *take* it anymore." The film is fictional, but the alienated millions are not—and the electronic church has identified their frustration.

In contrast, the mainline churches by and large have failed to identify with these people, or even to recognize they are there. Consequently, they have failed to minister to these new kinds of needs on the part of millions who live within reach of their ministry. In fact, the mainline churches are perceived by many to be a part of the problem—which is why they are called "dry, unfriendly, cold, dead, or dying," while the electronic-church ministers are perceived as those who care because "they answer my letters."

Second, the electronic church has fashioned a number of new models of interactive communication that creatively combine the technologies not only of television, satellite and cable, but also the computer-driven "personalized" letter, books, pamphlets, and study courses, the WATS-line telephone system, and regional and local groups used for referral and follow-up. Whole new systems of communication have been invented which the mainline churches thus far have almost totally ignored.

On the other hand, I believe the electronic church has failed miserably to adequately meet the needs of the people it has identified so accurately. It has failed for two reasons: because it has not taken seriously enough the demonic nature of general television, and because it has proceeded on an inadequate understanding of the nature of the Christian gospel.

First, the electronic church separates people from their own communities. Television already has substituted itself for many of the things we used to do communally: go to movies, attend local sports events and concerts, participate in clubs and meetings. For many people television has become a substitute for all of these activities. Now it is moving in on church participation. The electronic church undoubtedly does reinforce the religious convictions of many regular churchgoers. But for some it provides an easy and convenient substitute for face-to-face church attendance. The Annenberg research shows that at least 14% of electronic-church viewers admit that their viewing of the programs is a substitute for going to church.

The community of believers, the local church, is central to Christian faith and life. It is there that believers find the living embodiment of their faith among their neighbors. It is there that they confess their sins and find forgiveness and act out their faith and shore up one another when they slide back. The strategy of the electronic church is wrong to the extent that it would substitute a cathode tube and a phantom, nonpeople church for the church of real people with real needs and a faith to share in the midst of real lives.

Second, the electronic church is not good evangelism. As far back as 1978 a study by the Institute for American Church Growth indicated that mass evangelism is not an effective method of increasing church membership. Another revealed that most people come to church as a result of someone personally known to them or because of strong pastoral leadership.[9] Still other studies have shown that more than 80 out of 100 people who have joined the church in recent years came because of the word of a friend or relative. Far fewer than one out of 100 have come as a result of electronic evangelism.[10] The Annenberg research revealed that the viewers of the electronic-church programs are essentially those who already hold strong religious beliefs, and that the programs themselves function to confirm these beliefs. The programs reinforce the believer rather than convert the nonbeliever. Even from the point of view of the electronic church, these programs have more value as encouragement to the faithful than as evangelism to the world.

Third, the electronic church has become a captive to the commercial broadcasting system and its demands. Once broadcast preachers buy into commercial broadcasting, they have to follow the rules of the system: get more money to purchase more air time to reach more people to get more money—a never-ending cycle that is truly vicious. To capture and hold these ever-larger audiences, it is necessary to please an ever-larger part of the population—never offend, or challenge, or put the hard questions that biblical religion requires. Because of the financial demands of commercial broadcasting, the electronic church cannot afford to talk much about suffering, shared need, or requirements of the cross, about justice and humility, and giving one's self (not just one's checkbook) in love to one's neighbor.

Since the basic purpose of American commercial television is to attract an audience, it has cultivated a taste and expectation for instant gratification and simple answers. It doesn't handle complicated or challenging ideas very well. So in seeking huge audiences, the electronic-church preacher has to fall in line, providing trivial and superficial religion, a quick fix for people's anxieties. It therefore has to reduce the gospel to slogans—"Something good is going to happen to you today"—and to present a magical God whose favor can be bought by the highest bidder.

Fourth, the values implicit in most successful electronic-church programs are actually the values of the secular society it pretends to reject. Strip away the constantly repeated "praise God" and "Lord bless" and you discover the *real* values: material success, power, winning, security, wealth. This is true idolatry—to absorb the secular society's vision of success and self-centeredness and then justify it with a coating of verbal Christianity. This is in effect selling indulgences—a return to the very evils against which the Protestant Reformation rebelled some four centuries ago. The electronic church feeds America's growing alienation and narcissism, its "me-ism." "Me and my TV religion" fits neatly with "Me and my TV."

Fifth, the electronic church is driving religious diversity off the air. In their eagerness to get an audience, the radio and TV preachers have been willing to pay for air time—time which should be available free, as a public service to religious groups in every community. As short a time ago as 1959, 47% of broadcast religion was "sustaining," that is, available free to local and national churches. Today approximately 8% is available without charge; the rest is available to the highest bidder, without regard to whether the program relates to the needs and interests of the community.

But if money now becomes the only basis for access of any kind— religious, educational, political—to radio and television outlets, within a few years only the largest and wealthiest electronic evangelists (and teachers and politicians) will be able to stay on the air. Instead of remaining a free and independent institution, religion (and education and politics) can become just one more handmaiden of the secular commercial society.

Conclusions

The electronic church is great show business, a terrific audience grabber, and very much in tune with the times. But its popularity is more a sign that it has become just a part of TV's entertainment package with a religious gloss than that it is the good news of the Christian faith.

Therefore, so far as the mainline churches are concerned, if they can't beat 'em, they shouldn't join 'em, because, fortunately, the mainline denominations have an alternative which is unique, nationwide, and highly biblical: the local church.

If local mainline churches in America were to begin taking the needs of the American people as seriously as the electronic church now does, and if they began to meet those needs in fundamental ways, we might see a national revival unparalleled in our history.

New styles of worship, new forms of community, new approaches to communication will be required. But the local church is the place where this must take place, in face-to-face, long-term involvement of people with each other. The gospel simply cannot meet people's basic needs for recognition, involvement, worthiness, growth, and, indeed, for salvation, without person-to-person interaction over a long period of time.

Community is essential to humanity. But the advent of the technological era is requiring us to redefine some of the ways by which community exists, and to fashion communication processes which include the feedback and mutuality essential to community and to the life of its members. At the same time, our theology requires us to consider not only what the churches *can* do in the use of television, but also what they *should* do. Too often the religious response has been to ignore one or the other of these demands, and thus either to retreat into the irrelevancy of purity, or else to embrace uncritically the tools and powers of society.

In the next chapter we will consider some communication strategies that attempt to avoid both of these dangers, and suggest what the churches can and should be doing, both in terms of television production and in terms of dealing with the structures of the television industry itself, in ways that are both relevant to the needs of the culture and faithful to the demands of the gospel.

SEVEN

STRATEGIES FOR MAINLINE CHURCHES

To communicate the Gospel means putting it before
the people so that they are able to decide for or
against it. The Christian Gospel is a matter of decision.
It is to be accepted or rejected. All that we who
communicate this Gospel can do is make possible a
genuine decision.

Paul Tillich, *Theology of Culture*

In Chapter 2 we saw how religious groups with differing theologies respond in different ways to the challenge of television. In Chapters 5 and 6 we considered the electronic-church preachers who have adopted a "Christ of culture" response which uses the techniques of the world of the technological era, a world of means that values technique ("whatever works is good") over human values.

There is within the Christian tradition a response which rejects the accommodation of religion to the worldview of the media, but also refuses to reject the media altogether. It is a response which calls for a multiple relationship to the media, sometimes dealing with it as partner, occasionally as the enemy, often as antagonist, certainly always as one to be befriended wherever possible. This alternative can be discerned in both the Niebuhrian models of "Christ transforming culture" and "Christ and culture in paradox." It is a response of *creative transformation.*

Creative Transformation of the Mass Media

Creative transformation rejects both the "Christ against culture" and the "Christ of culture" stances, because the first entails renouncing all meaningful relationships with the world and the second uncritically embraces the world. The essence of the Christian ethic is to be in the world but not of it—to recognize the vitality and goodness in the world while at the same time maintaining sufficient critical distance to seek its transformation or, in theological terms, its redemption from sin. Such a position deals both with the ultimate worth of individuals and the reality of sin in individuals and their institutions and political and economic structures. It understands that the kingdom of God is not something (or someplace) which we can expect to "bring in" at a particular time or place, but rather something both within our midst (Luke 17:22), and at the same time to be sought (Matt. 6:33), to be seen (Mark 9:1), to be entered into (Mark 10:23).

This orientation means that a distinctly religious contribution to programming in television is one in which people are helped to grow toward a deeper and more mature understanding of themselves, their society, and their world. It rejects the message of the electronic church, because it proclaims that the old Shibboleths, the old authorities, and the old system in which people waited for the church to tell them what to do, are no longer valid and are indeed dangerous in our society. It implies helping men and women, in Bonhoeffer's phrase, to come of age. At the same time, it means proclaiming that God commits to the poor, the downtrodden, the unfree, and that service in today's world requires whatever is necessary to help humanize those who are denied a full human life.

Programming Strategies

Creative transformation relates to television at two levels. One level of relationship is *programming*. The objective here is to develop programs on TV which, within the very midst of TV's expressions of secular worldview and power, nevertheless attempt to illuminate the human condition, to ask meaningful religious questions, to rediscover religious truths, and to find new religious vocabulary which can have meaning and power for multitudes of men and women today.

Such productions can have very little success in "worldly" terms, that is, in relation to audience size, income for stations and networks, or the creation of national celebrities and media events which can be merchandized. The financial constraints of television as presently structured simply reject programming which is too costly, complicated, or disturbing.

This programming approach is really a kind of subversive activity, seeking out the most vulnerable points within the mass media's powerful and virtually monolithic structure, and insinuating itself in ways that are sufficiently in line with the media's own expectations that it will not be readily rejected. It employs a kind of *media jujitsu* which turns the media's own massive weight and ponderous structure to the advantage of small, poor, but creative and liberating programming.

For example, it is encouraging to recognize that there are literally hundreds of people within the mass-media industries who are frustrated with the limitations imposed upon them. Men and women in the secular media often are more sensitive to the needs and the issues of the world than are church leaders. Within limits, they can write and direct and produce programs which reflect their own consciences rather than the demands of the system. They are potential colleagues in our attempts at media jujitsu. And even where common ground cannot be found, our theology calls us to deal with the secular media as the place to which Christ sent his disciples. Unfortunately, the churches have not been very successful at working in this area. Christian evangelism must become more sophisticated and creative in working with and encouraging the people in the secular media.

A few examples of the moral jujitsu or subversive creative approach may help clarify what can be—and is being—done. For years the Paulist Fathers in Los Angeles have given the lucrative Humanitas Award—a $25,000 prize for the best long-form scripts, $15,000 for one-hour scripts, $10,000 for half-hour scripts, $10,000 for those in the children's category. Such substantial amounts encourage television writers, in effect, to spend more time than they could normally afford, in order to write a quality script. The simple fact is that it takes more time and effort to write a scene which deals sensitively with human beings than it does to write a scene describing a car chase. The Humanitas Award and others such as the National Council of Churches' annual Film Awards, the Christophers awards to productions "affirming the highest value of the human spirit," and the Southern Baptist Abe Lincoln Awards, encourage producers, directors, and writers to devote time to their craft which the media industry itself, because of its profit considerations, simply does not reward.

Another point of vulnerability in the system is the industry's own defensiveness and sense of guilt which often is expressed in management's desire to produce a few quality programs even at the expense of achieving maximum profits, in order to project a "quality" or public-service image to the populace. Many stations, groups, or networks regularly purchase expensive full-page ads in *Broadcasting* magazine, the industry's bible, in order to trumpet the most trivial award. Broadcasters even create their own spots to tell the public how public-minded they are. In an industry making such large profits by using a public resource, the industry's attempts to prove how public-spirited they are provide excellent leverage for moral jujitsu on the part of public-interest groups, including the churches.

Another example is the programs which all three commercial networks have provided to the major faith groups since the beginning of television, based on their historical commitment to providing an opportunity for religious expression in the society. Unfortunately, these programs have never had the real funding and promotion they deserved, again because of the commercial base of the networks. Nevertheless, they have garnered considerable audiences. During the 12-year period from 1970 to 1981, the NBC-TV series of religious specials had an average Nielsen rating of 2.31, or an average audience of slightly more than 3 million persons for each program. This is an impressive audience, considering the fact that the programs were never shown at prime time but only on Sunday afternoons, were moved about when sports programs took precedence, were never seriously advertised, and were shown on only about one-half of the NBC stations. While the networks want to be seen and known to have religious programs on the air, their economic demands can not allow such programs to become competitive to their profit-making shows.

The faith-group programs, representing Protestant, Catholics, and Jews, have consistently provided documentaries, dramas, and discussions which dealt with issues almost never touched by commercial broadcasting: the economic factors behind nuclear armaments; the issues behind draft evasion (during the Vietnam War); the real causes of worldwide starvation; and the problems of people who are ignored almost completely by the media, such as the aging who cannot live on their pensions, the unwed mothers, the farm workers who have no homes, the undocumented aliens whom we wish to employ but not pay, and refugees we are sending back to certain death in their own countries. Such programs as these have brought to the American people ethical questions about U.S. support of repressive regimes in the Philippines, in South Korea, in Chile, and in South Africa, long before they became "news" to the commercial media.

These programs have been produced by the networks for a variety of reasons. The FCC has occasionally raised an eyebrow in the direction of network public-service accountability, although, beginning in 1980, support from that direction almost ceased. The press sometimes raises questions about the broadcasters' program quality and public service, and from time to time has praised a particular network program. The leadership of the churches has maintained a modest presence, and the network executives have preferred to avoid a confrontation with such a large institution in society. Also, within the networks themselves, dedicated staff in the religion departments have fought valiantly for the survival and the quality of their programs.

Another example of moral jujitsu occurs where local church groups are able to get a religious perspective on the news originating from their local stations. Unfortunately, what most stations understand as "religious news" is limited to what is being discussed about institutional religion in the national news at the moment—abortion, politicized ministers, and so on—rather than a discussion of *all* the news from various religious perspectives. Nevertheless, a number of local councils of churches and other broad-based religious groups have managed to get a significant airing of news from a religious perspective on their local stations. The objective of this approach is not to present *the* religious view on a particular subject. Rather, the aim is to generate robust discussion and debate about the significant issues of the day from many different religious perspectives and viewpoints.

Reform Strategies

The second level of relationship to television occurs where religious groups work toward *reform* of the media, dealing with the political and social institutions as well, to bring about conditions which allow the media to achieve their highest potential. The objective here is to humanize the structures which govern the mass media, both by encouraging persons within the industry to "do well by doing good," and by insisting that the social and economic powers of the media must be counterbalanced by other kinds of power which express the concerns of citizens for the general welfare.

This requires generating countervailing powers, which usually takes two forms: political and economic. The political approach was used in the struggles of public-interest groups, with church organizations in the lead, to achieve media reform during the 1960s and 1970s. In many cases these struggles were successful. Laws or regulations were established which set the rules by which the entire media industry had to abide.

For example, as the result of law suits instituted by public-interest groups, the courts held that whenever broadcasters present a particular point of view on a matter of public importance, they also must provide opportunities for opposing viewpoints to be presented. This Fairness Doctrine has become the foundation of free speech on radio and television, and it has prevented many of the more blatant attempts by some broadcasters to use the public airwaves as nothing more than a sounding board for their own special views and interests. Political action requires considerable expertise on the part of church groups. It also requires money and time. But in the complex society in which we live, such intervention often is the only way for citizens to make their moral and ethical concerns matter.

The economic approach is even more complex and difficult, but it is also even more fundamental. As long as economic gain is the sole consideration among broadcasters, we cannot expect to have television which approaches communication in terms of meeting the needs of the citizens for information and expression. Changes in the present system are possible, although they are exceedingly difficult because of the political power wielded by the broadcasting industry itself. One of the central economic factors encouraging this power is the tax laws which allow businesses to write off advertising as a business expenditure. This single provision in effect subsidizes the media industries by hundreds of millions of dollars each year. Also, while the broadcast industry is provided with a government-protected monopoly over the use of a particular frequency, it is taxed as if it were an ordinary business, subject to all of the risks other businesses face through genuine competition. If broadcasters were required to pay even a modest fee for their licenses, the revenues could provide a well-funded public broadcasting system, and citizens would begin to benefit from the special advantages they have accorded to the broadcasters.

Another kind of economic intervention can come through direct citizen action. Since the advertising base is the foundation on which television is based, citizen action directed toward the advertiser tends to have considerable leverage.

For example, stockholder action is a strategy in which owners of stock in a company which advertises on TV seek to get the company to adopt a policy saying they will not place advertising on violent programs. Perhaps the action could be directed at instructing company officers to support public broadcasting or a particular kind of children's program. Such action is consistent with the free enterprise system in which we live. If corporations profit from what people decide to buy, and if they adjust their production and advertising policies according to buyers' preferences and the interests of stockholders, then they also are amenable to what the public refuses to buy or what their stockholders establish as policy, and should be expected to adjust their production and advertising plans to take into account buyer and stockholder preferences.

This dual approach to the mass media—production and reform, co-operation and citizen action—exemplifies the concept of creative transformation. It recognizes the ambiguities and paradoxical nature of the church's role within a system that is full of powers which potentially corrupt everything they touch, including the church. At the same time it acts in the belief that testifying to the good news is a mandate that cannot be avoided, and that—potentially—faith and action based on the liberating gospel can indeed transform structures built upon human sin and pride.

Creative transformation of the mass media, both from within and from the outside, is a necessary objective of the churches as they face the challenges of the technological era.

Television as Preparation for the Gospel

H. Richard Niebuhr gave a description of the nature of the church and the world which has remarkable relevance to the current situation facing religion in its uneasy and ambivalent relationship to the world of television in America:

> The Church lives and defines itself in action vis-à-vis the world. World, however, is not object of Church as God is. World, rather, is companion of the Church, a community something like itself with which it lives before God. . . .
> The world is the community of those before God who feel rejected

by God and reject him; again, it is the community of those who do not know God and seem not to be known by him; or, it is the community of those who, knowing God, do not worship him. In all cases it is the community to which the Church addresses itself with the gospel, to which it gives an account of what it has seen and heard in divine revelation, which it invites the world to come and see and hear.

The world is the community to which Christ comes and to which he sends his disciples. On the other hand, the world is the community of those who are occupied with temporal things. When, in its sense of rejection, it is preoccupied with these temporal matters it is the world of idolatry and becomes foe of the Church. When it is occupied with them as gifts of God—whether or not the consciousness of grace becomes explicit—it is the partner of the Church, doing what the Church, concerned with the nontemporal, cannot do; knowing what Church as such cannot know.[1]

One implication of this complex and dynamic relationship is that the message of the gospel cannot today be a *direct* proclamation of religious truths as they are given in the Bible and in Christian tradition. The thoughtful person today has profound doubts precisely about the authority of the Bible, the Christian tradition, and the church itself. For these reasons, if we were asked whether TV can be "used for mission" today, the answer would be no. But if we were asked whether TV can be expected to confront people with serious religious questions, the answer would be yes. TV—commercial, not "religious" TV—can confront a president with Watergate, confront Congress with Nicaragua, confront the nation with South Africa. TV can sensitize, enlarge our vision, make us aware, ask the moral questions—and doing this is a form of mission.

But because of television's inherent characteristics as a mass medium—one-way, resistant to feedback, incapable of dialog—and its acquired social characteristic as society's sales agent—simplistic, gratifying, trivial—it is best suited to the role of preparation for the gospel, or *pre-evangelism*. This means we cannot expect it to *be* the gospel, but we can expect it to help prepare people to ask the right questions, to understand more fully who they are, and to accept the Christian worldview.

Preparation for the gospel involves three steps. First it requires us to find and describe what Tillich called the "boundary situations," that is, those points where modern men and women reach the limits of their human existence, where they sense they are alienated from society and other people, or feel a lack of personal meaning, or fear being useless and having no worth.[2] These symptoms are described by psychologists as the root of the disorientation many people face today in their lives, although people manage to cover over and obscure them as a part of their elaborate defense mechanisms. The first task of authentic Christian communication is to help people face the reality of these self-doubts and to enable them to ask serious questions about the meaning of their existence.

Paulo Friere applied this concept to basic education. His approach seeks first of all to get people to accept the fact that *something is wrong*. Friere was successful in reaching the peasants of Latin America because he insisted that, first of all, they explore what is wrong in their lives and why they tolerate it. When people are able to examine those "boundaries" which they had always accepted without question, they are then both motivated and equipped to move on to analysis and action.[3]

The second step is then possible—to affirm those men and women who have been able to take these "boundary situations" seriously, facing them and dealing with them creatively and with faith. It is only when people are able to face the fact that they have *no* permanent, guaranteed security that the claim of the gospel can be made—and our communication must state this unequivocally. As Tillich says, "Protestantism must proclaim the judgment that brings assurance by depriving us of all security; the judgment that declares us whole in the disintegration and cleavage of soul and community; the judgment that affirms our having truth in the very absence of truth; the judgment that reveals the meaning of our life in the situation in which all the meaning of life has disappeared."[4]

On television, affirmation can come through the news (Selma, Manila, South Africa), through biography (Dietrich Bonhoeffer, Gandhi, Martin Luther King Jr., C. S. Lewis), through drama ("A Man for All Seasons," "Who's Afraid of Virginia Wolfe?" "The Burning Bed"), or through documentaries (Dr. Kübler-Ross on children facing death, the sanctuary movement, antinuclear protests, Archbishop Tutu). The purpose of all of these religious messages is to make the spiritual assertion that our lives are devoid of security, truth, and meaning unless and until we become a part of God—in other words, until we become part of that which is really real.

Third, Christian communication must finally witness to the power of the Christian faith in Jesus Christ. This means witnessing that the Christian faith is effective both in the lives of individuals and in the life of the total community. Christian communication needs to find its rootage, its raw stuff, from within the experiences of daily life, and then attempt to show in what way this ordinary, day-by-day existence has ultimate meaning. Again, Tillich suggests the way:

> It is not so important to produce new liturgies as it is to penetrate into the depths of what happens day by day, in labor and industry, in marriage and friendship, in social regions and recreation, in meditation and tranquility, in the unconscious and the conscious life. To elevate all this into the light of the eternal is the great task of (church communication), and not to reshape a tradition traditionally.[5]

On television this is best done by telling *stories*—stories which reveal what the gospel means for Christians (rather than for everyone). These stories should be "models of hope," that is, examples of real people and their real responses in faith to the challenges to meaning and worth in their lives. They become particularly revelatory when they tell the story of some*one* and what the gospel means to that person.

To repeat, this communication, as creative and as relevant as we hope it may be, cannot actually *give* people the gospel. It can only *prepare* people to receive the gospel. It can prepare people by exposing them to the ultimate questions about what is "really real," and by giving them insights which will help them live in their daily lives in such a way that those lives will have meaning, truth, and security.

But if television can only help people ask the right questions, where do people go to find the right answers? Once again we return to the place where people come face-to-face with other people who have the same questions, who have been working on the answers, who have discovered answers only to lose them and who need to rediscover them once again. We return to the church.

It is within the environment of the church that people can discover and rediscover the answers, where they can assist others to do so, where they can together celebrate the fact that these answers make sense to *them*. The function of the mass media is to become a sign, as it were, an arrow pointing in the direction of the church. This signing is important, because often people do not know that they have lost their way, or, if they know, they do not know where to find the way again. The Christian message in the mass media is that "We are all lost, and here is where you can find the way."

As we work at this creative programming in the media, we must do it in ways that are particular rather than universal, specific rather than general, real rather than ideal, and personal-in-the-mass rather than mass appeal. It is important to remember that there literally is no such thing as a mass audience; there are only ways of looking at individuals in the mass. When mass communication is employed in the sense we are talking about it here, *there is no mass;* there are only massive numbers of *individuals*. And it is to these individuals—as individuals, or perhaps small groups of two or three—that we speak.

Therefore, our communication must tell what the gospel means for Christians rather than what it means for all men and women, everywhere, for all time. We must tell what *we*—or, really, what *I*—think it means and can mean for *you*. It pursues its inquiry by recalling the story of the Christian life and by analyzing what Christians see from their point of view of history and of faith. Russ Reid, a Christian deeply involved in media, puts it this way:

> You see, when I say "Christ is the answer" I really don't have to own that. I can say it, but it doesn't say anything about what Christ has done for me. And it doesn't really tell you how He's the answer, because if you are intelligent at all, you'll say, Well, what is the question? The only way you can communicate what Jesus Christ can do in a man's life is by saying "once I was blind, now I see." Now, there is something that happened to me, and others can identify with that.[6]

Of course, commercial television tends to reject most—though not all—of this kind of programming, which means that the church's involvement in the mass media is necessarily limited both by the natural strictures of the medium itself and by the artificially imposed rejection of the message which is inherent in its profit-motivated structure. Rather than debase the essential gospel message to the point of caricature, the option for the church is to continue to *be* the church so that its message will remain clear and distinctive, and to use the mass media where it can (including the subversive and jujitsu approaches). But

Christians ought not feel that they have to "be on television" simply because television is a powerful communication environment, any more than Christians felt they had to be cheering in the stands of the Circus Maximus during Caesar's day simply because that was where the rich and powerful were in the first century.

There is one additional production strategy for mainline churches—to employ the newer "narrowcast" media for religious education and the encouragement of the faithful already in the church.

Narrowcasting

The local church has far greater opportunity to use the new communication media to reach relatively small, segmented, and specialized audiences than it has to use truly mass media which have such inherent bias against its message. The narrowcast media include cable TV, videocassettes, videodiscs, local point-to-point broadcasting, low-power TV stations, subcarrier frequencies of FM radio and TV, and direct mail. These media are relatively efficient and effective, and while they are limited in their scope, they permit the churches to use them in ways which are in keeping with religious values rather than simply meeting the utilitarian demands of the new technology.

A significant opportunity awaits those churches which develop a cooperative plan to provide *educational materials* on these narrowcast media. For example, a master teacher could help every fourth grade volunteer church-school teacher in the entire community, each week, as they prepare their teaching lesson. And, via satellite, this same service could be made available nationwide for almost the same cost as in a single community. However, this kind of media usage requires both local and national churches to cooperate in their religious education programs to a degree they have not yet been willing to do. For churches to use media nationwide on a truly cost-effective basis, they must become "denomination-blind" to an extent not yet manifest. One value of the mass media in the society is that they may force churches to recognize that they have much more in common than they think. Cooperation in the use of media can be a valuable start in engendering true ecumenism.

The potential for using narrowcast media for education in the churches is large, and to date almost completely unexplored. Courses for ministers and lay leaders in Bible study, church history, Christian doctrine, ethics, and other subjects, are simply awaiting the creativity of the right seminary or school of religion to develop them. Until now only the Southern Baptist Sunday School Board has pioneered in providing their church schools with materials via a leased satellite which feeds local cable systems throughout the country, and, in some cases, is picked up directly by local churches.

Cable is an excellent way to provide very low cost, simple production coverage of worship services for the elderly, the shut-ins, the hospital patients, and people who are "shopping" for a church. Hundreds of churches have found they can purchase a line to their local cable head-end and, with almost no equipment other than a single camera, feed the morning worship service over their local cable channel. Often this can be done without charge. If the local cable company is not cooperative, a consortium of churches should seek to get the city to require at least some "public access"; and this should be done at the time of the cable company's franchise renewal.

The objective of local cable programming is to provide a service to those not otherwise able to attend church. The objective ought *not* to be "broadcasting" the church to the community. Once a church becomes engaged in competition with commercial channels for audience it immediately becomes swept up in high costs, slick production, and a need to please the audience "out there." While there is a place for high quality worship services broadcast on true mass media, such programs require a great amount of careful planning and considerable cost, and are tailored to meeting the need for a kind of national worship experience in which those not in church can participate. Such programs as "The National Radio Pulpit" and "The Protestant Hour" on radio, and Robert Schuller's "Hour of Power" on television are purposely designed to reach a national audience with a worship experience. A local church is in competition with these national programs and the whole panoply of secular programming when it attempts to "broadcast" to a "mass" audience. Unless the church is prepared to engage in a costly, massive, and time-consuming activity, it should limit its TV ministry to reaching those not in church; cable is a cost-effective way to do this.

Several alternative media can achieve the same objective, but at additional cost. Videocassettes can be made of the worship service and taken to individuals in their homes, hospitals, nursing facilities, and so on. The program can be placed on a low-power television station, if one is available in their viewing area, or point-to-point broadcast services can be purchased for feeding to hospitals and other institutions. Some local public broadcasting stations have a low-cost "broadcast" to points which have special antennas, and they might make this available as a public service. Also, a simple audiotape recorder can be used to tape the service, with church visitors taking the "service" with them to shut-ins. Finally, some FM stations make available their subcarrier to public groups, for broadcast tapes of the worship service or other program especially designed for the shut-in.

Direct mail is another medium which the mainline churches have ignored at their peril. The slick and cynical "personalized" mail of the electronic church has tended to discourage others from using the technique. However, direct mail, using computer technology, has great potential for allowing local churches to reach parishioners who have special interests in missions, or religious education, or evangelism, or a Bible-study course. Computers are assisting many churches in handling their mailing lists and in compiling lists of small interest groups which can be given resources from a national base.

Computers, while not a narrowcast medium, strictly speaking, nevertheless must be considered by local churches for use as a helpful tool in allowing special-interest groups to aggregate around topics of interest, for news and information, and for financial accounting and transfer. Already there are numerous experimental computer networks within various denominations, including Presbynet, UMCOMM Teletalk, the United Church Christnet, and the Lutheran RELIGION-ONLINE.

Creating Community

The purpose of narrowcasting is to create and to maintain *community* within cities and towns but also within the local churches themselves. The rebuilding of community is essential in a time of media-induced isolation and fragmentation, and in this effort the churches will of necessity find common cause with other community agencies.

For example, local point-to-point communication is beginning to develop as a communication tool for maintaining local community. At least one public broadcasting station, WITF-TV in Harrisburg, Pennsylvania, is creating a community-development process which helps people discuss issues of common interest, and, in effect, to re-create community. This station has put together a consortium of businesses, schools and colleges, churches, hospitals, and community agencies, which already is helping reeducate people when they are displaced by "technology," helping them find new jobs, training leaders in the areas of community services, and facilitating the discussion of common community projects. The objective is to humanize the community. The churches have a similar objective, and they should be leading the way in the innovation of such community development programs, which can involve both the mass media and the narrowcast media.

Media Education

Fred Friendly, originator and producer of Edward R. Murrow's "See It Now" and a former president of CBS News, once said: "We live today in a world where it's what you *don't* know that can kill you."[7]

More people depend on television than any other medium for their news and information about what is going on in the world. And television has become our prime storyteller, the creator of the images and narratives which, taken altogether, provide us with a worldview which seriously competes with the real world of direct experience. Therefore, it is becoming increasingly critical *what we decide to pay attention to.*

One of the new facts of our time is the enormous information overload. Thousands of persons devote their entire professional lives simply to getting our attention, inventing shorter TV spots, more urgent-looking direct mail, songs with built-in commercials, movies with built-in songs, and TV graphics that move, turn, and dance. And for every new trick devised to get us to look, we develop new internal mechanisms to switch off the overload in order to protect our sanity.

But in learning to tune out the intrusive and the blatant, we also tend to ignore some of the still small voices, those hints and nuances of news and relationships and information that can tell us what really is going on. Thus our defenses threaten to make us insensitive. Learning what to pay attention to has become essential not only to survival but also to human growth and nurture.

For these reasons, media education is now an essential tool. It now must become central to the curriculum in our kindergartens, schools, and colleges, if we hope to live in a society where the average citizens can cope with the barrage of images which daily comes into their lives, and where what they *do* know will help them survive.

In the churches, a major role of the Christian educator (and that includes the minister and lay teacher) is to help people understand what the media are really saying and doing to them—and how they can avoid being taken in by its worldview. The churches must plan systematically to expose every parishioner to the biases and distorted values systems of our culture in the light of the prophetic visions of the Old Testament and the harsh demands of the New.

Some successful first steps already are in place. The Television Awareness Training program, pioneered by the Media Action Research Center in New York City, and funded by a coalition of Protestant denominations, has certified hundreds of trainers across the nation over the past decade. An interdenominational curriculum series, called "Growing with Television," also is available from the half-dozen Protestant publishing houses which helped print it. This 13-week unit has separate curriculum for early and late primaries, junior and senior highs, and adults.

However, most church leaders, both nationally and locally, still tend to view television as if it were merely an entertaining diversion which sometimes keeps people away from their churches, rather than as an alternative religion which is wooing people into a whole new way of thinking about, and living in, our world. Real media education will not become effective in the churches until it has penetrated the thinking of every theologian, pastor, and parishioner—and this calls for a change in orientation in every theological school.

Media education does not stop at the teaching of visual grammar and an analysis of imagery, although these are fundamental. Media education also needs to help people ask key questions about the way television functions as an institution in society.

How do the media change the ways we think, make decisions, vote, spend money, treat others? How can we reform the media so that they will meet the genuine human needs of the society? The answer to these questions can be understood more clearly if we investigate three of the most significant ethical issues involving television today: violence; censorship and regulation; and the international implications of American media policies. It is to these issues that we now turn.

EIGHT

MEDIA VIOLENCE IS HAZARDOUS TO YOUR HEALTH

What is honored in a country will be cultivated there.

Plato (4th c. B.C.)

Violence and Television

The problem of violence on television and its effects in the society is one of the most revealing examples of the complex relationship between media and culture. For this reason, we will need to examine the issue in some detail. First, we will look at violence in America in general and ask how television has been related to the growth of violence over the past three decades. Second, we will examine the research, inquiring about the effect TV violence has on real-life violence. Then, in the next chapter, we will look at the television industry itself and ask, Who are the players and what are the factors in determining how much violence there is on TV? Finally, we will look at some "middle axioms" and ask, What specific action can citizens take to deal with the situation?

It is a fact that Americans are more prone to violence than are any other people of the industrialized nations of the world. Between 1963 and 1973, while the war in Vietnam was taking 46,212 lives, firearms in America killed 84,644 civilians. If the United States had the same homicide rate as Japan, our 1966 death toll from guns would have been 32 instead of 6,855. In the last 50 years the rape rate in the United States has increased 700%, on a per capita basis. In 1980 there were 8 handgun murders in England and 10,012 in the United States.[1] During the last 30 years our homicide rate per capita has increased almost

100%. Between 1974 and 1983, the number per capita of aggravated assaults increased 6%, forcible rape 26%, robbery 2%, and child abuse 48%.[2]

For years people have asked whether the amount of violence portrayed on American movie and TV screens has anything to do with the growing violence on our streets and in our homes.

As early as the 1950s Congress held hearings on the possible negative effects of television. When Senators Dodd and Kefauver expressed concern over the role of TV shows in the increasing rates of juvenile delinquency and crime, industry representatives immediately promised to reduce violence while simultaneously denying any evidence of harmful effects. Yet from the mid-50s to mid-60s, television violence increased markedly.

In the summer of 1967 Americans discovered themselves to be in the grip of unprecedented violence. Troops and bombs were being shipped at an accelerating rate to a bloody undeclared war in Vietnam. Racial disorders were rocking the cities. During a two-week period in July whole sections of Detroit and Newark were bombed, burned, and vandalized. Martial law was enforced and curfews were established. National Guardsmen and heavily armed police patrolled the streets. Citizens looted liquor and appliance stores, bringing their booty home in liberated shopping carts. In some 75 disorders that summer, 83 deaths were reported. The overwhelming majority of persons killed or injured were blacks.

On July 26, 1967, President Johnson established a National Advisory Commission on Civil Disorders. He gave it substantial staff and budget, and charged it with finding out what had happened, why, and what could be done to prevent similar violence in the future.

In March 1968, the commission issued a 608-page report to the president.[3] The commission laid much of the blame for the crisis on the mass media. It found that although the media tried to give a balanced and factual account of the events of the summer of 1967, they tended overall to exaggerate "both good and bad events." Television, in particular, was found to have presented violence in simplistic terms—depicting "a visual three-way alignment of Negroes, white bystanders, and public officials or enforcement agents," which tended to create the impression that the riots were predominantly racial confrontations between blacks and whites, while other factors such as economic and political frustration were pushed into the background. The commission found that television, more than any other medium, failed to present and analyze in sufficient extent and depth the basic reasons for the disorders.

But the commission did not find a *causal* relationship between television coverage and the disorders. With the exception of the live helicopter coverage of the Watts riots in California, no evidence was found that the media actually caused riots.

The national unrest persisted. In early 1968 Martin Luther King Jr. was shot and killed in Memphis; then Robert Kennedy was assassinated in Los Angeles. On June 10, 1968, President Johnson established a new National Commission on the Causes and Prevention of Violence, headed by Dr. Milton S. Eisenhower, brother of the former president and president emeritus of Johns Hopkins University. It was charged "to undertake a penetrating search . . . into our national life, our past as well as our present, our traditions as well as our institutions, our culture, our customs and our laws."

A major focus of the Eisenhower Commission was the relationship between violence and the mass media. Its report revealed that in network drama:

- 8 out of every 10 plays contain violence;
- violence occurs at the rate of 7 times an hour;
- there are 600 separate acts of TV violence per week;
- half of the leading characters act violently; and
- one out of every 10 leading characters kills somebody.

The report said that the amount of on-the-air violence in 1968 had actually increased slightly over 1967, despite growing concern in the Congress and the nation. It commissioned studies which described the characteristics of TV violence:

- Physical pain is not a visible result of most violent acts.
- Witnesses to violence are usually passive spectators.
- Young adults are most likely to kill; middle-aged persons are most likely to get killed.
- Foreigners and nonwhites are more likely to commit violence than are white Americans.
- In committing violent acts, the question of legality or illegality seldom arises.

"On the whole," the study said, "it is safe to conclude that violence is rarely shown as unacceptable."

On September 23, 1969, the final media report was issued. It noted that advertisers were spending $2.5 billion each year in the belief that television *does* influence human behavior. With regard to children, the report noted that while they turn to TV for mere entertainment, actually a process of "observational learning" takes place. It found that the younger the child, the more he or she identified with the program and learned from it. Also, the less well-integrated adolescents are, the more they bring what they see on TV into their real-life world.

The report completely rejected the "cathartic" argument, that is, the idea that TV violence merely drains off the aggressive tendencies of persons. Instead, it found the reverse to be true: "the vast majority of experimental studies on this question have found that observed violence stimulates aggressive behavior, rather than the opposite."

In its summary, the commission stated: "Violence on television encourages violent forms of behavior, and fosters moral and social values about violence in daily life which are unacceptable in a civilized society."

The commission then specifically proposed to broadcasters that

(1) there be an over-all reduction in programs that require or contain violence;

(2) violence in children's cartoons—except for the fanciful "Popeye" kinds of violence—be eliminated;

(3) crime, Western, and adventure stories containing serious violence be scheduled only after 9 P.M. (as was done in England and elsewhere in Europe);

(4) provision be made for adequate funding of the Corporation for Public Broadcasting so it can develop educational, cultural, and dramatic programming not provided by commercial broadcasting.

It made two recommendations to parents: that they

(1) supervise their children's viewing; and

(2) express public approval and disapproval of programs to their local stations and national networks.

The report concluded: "Television entertainment based on violence may be effective merchandising, but it is an appalling way to serve the 'public interest, convenience and necessity.' "[4]

One would have thought that, given the commission's thoroughness and unambiguous findings, major changes would have taken place at the networks and stations. But it was not to be.

The Eisenhower Commission had no power to enforce its recommendations, and the broadcasting industry resisted the conclusions of the commission and attacked its findings as based on insufficient evidence. At the same time, network presidents solemnly proclaimed that violence *was* being reduced and that children's programming was being improved.

In 1964, the U.S. Surgeon General, acting as chief U.S. Public Health Officer, had issued a finding that cigarette smoking was a dangerous health hazard. In response to this official finding, a private-citizen suit initiated in 1967, followed by a ruling by the Federal Communication Commission and finally by Federal Law in 1971, forced cigarette advertising off the air, at a cost to the broadcasters of $150 million in advertising revenues.

Senator John O. Pastore, chairman of the Communication Subcommittee, decided to try a similar tactic with TV violence. In 1969 he requested the Surgeon General, Dr. Jesse Steinfeld, to appoint a committee to conduct a study "which will establish scientifically insofar as possible what harmful effects, if any, these [televised crime and violence] programs have on children." Congress provided a $1 million budget.

The explosive implications of the Surgeon General's study did not escape the broadcasting industry. When the study began, the Surgeon General's office was pressured into giving the three commercial networks veto power of approval over *all* 12 members of the committee, a prerogative which CBS declined, but which both NBC and ABC used to veto seven of the prospective members. Later there was considerable disagreement within the commission as to the exact wording of certain key passages in the report, and a number of professors who conducted the basic studies publicly complained that the committee's final report understated the cause-and-effect relationships they had found between media violence and aggressive behavior.

Nevertheless, Dr. Steinfeld testified in 1972 at a Senate hearing that the study had unearthed "sufficient data" to establish a *causal relationship* between watching television violence and aggressive behavior. Said Dr. Steinfeld: "My professional response . . . is that the broadcasters should be put on notice. The overwhelming consensus and the unanimous Scientific Advisory Committee's report indicate that television violence, indeed, does have an adverse effect on certain members of our society."[5]

Dean Burch, who was chairman of the Federal Communications Commission at the time, indicated at the hearings that the broadcasting industry's response should be "immediate and decisive," and that their response should include sharp reductions in "all gratuitous and needless violence" in the programs children watch, and "the creation of substantial amounts of new diversified programming, not just the usual diet of cartoons, to open the eyes and minds of young viewers." However, according to the "Violence Profile" conducted annually at the request of Congress by Dr. George Gerbner of the University of Pennsylvania's Annenberg School of Communications, there was no significant change in the level of violence in television throughout the 1970s.

The industry responded by challenging Gerbner's Violence Profile. Writing in the *Journal of Broadcasting* in 1977, David M. Blank, head of research at CBS, contended that Gerbner's study defined violence too broadly by including cartoons and slapstick violence and that it counted some single acts of violence as multiple. Sampling only one week a year is inadequate, said Blank, who also claimed that Gerbner's "risk ratio" measures relative rather than absolute victimization.[6] Annenberg countered that comic content (such as cartoons) is indeed a highly effective form of conveying serious lessons; that when a new person or agent enters a scene a "single" violent episode becomes "multiple"; that a six-week analysis made by the researchers revealed the same general results as the one-week sample; and that the risk ratio validly takes into account the fear that potential victims (such as young women) have when viewing violent television.[7]

But broadcasters continued to insist that the research on the behavioral effects of TV violence was inconclusive. Gene Mater, a CBS spokesperson, told a Congressional hearing in 1981: "I think our figures, our studies, and lots of other studies [show] that there is no unanimity . . . .In other words, [today] there are more defined issues, and more people who definitely believe, more social scientists who believe, there is no cause-and-effect relationship between televised violence and social behavior."[8]

Mater cautioned against making television the only object of concern when seeking solutions to the problem of violence, arguing that "with this single focus we ignore many of the root causes of societal ills," and neglect elements other than media which influence our lives—the home, school, church, and peer groups.

CBS prepared a memorandum entitled "Research on Television Violence: The Fact of Dissent," for the 1981 congressional hearings. It quoted Dr. Eli Rubenstein, the former vice-chairman of the original surgeon general's report, regarding the lack of unanimity among the researchers: ". . . the views today of studies done in the past decade have apparently served to support diametrically opposing conclusions."[9]

But research continued, and in May of 1982, the National Institute for Mental Health released the findings of a 10-year follow-up on the Surgeon General's 1972 Study entitled *Television and Behavior:* "After ten more years of research, the consensus among most of the research community is that violence on television does lead to aggressive behavior by children and teenagers who watch the programs."[10]

The report noted that "not all children become aggressive, of course," but that "the correlations between violence and aggression are positive," indeed as strong as "any other variable behavior that has been measured." Conversely, the study found "children can learn to be altruistic, friendly and self-controlled by looking at television programs depicting such behavior patterns."[11]

A group of social scientists who analyzed the NIMH study for the *Public Opinion Quarterly* stated: "We are convinced, in general, that the NIMH report presents a reasonable summary of current knowledge about television, its effects and its potential. . . . The report convincingly takes us beyond the 'no effects' era of Klapper (1960). . . . Evidence of negative effects is apparent. What is missing in the NIMH reports, as in nearly all television research, are mechanisms for going from the evidence produced by television researchers to changes in television practice."[12]

Thus by 1982 the overwhelming weight of research had demonstrated various degrees of relationship between violence in the media and violent behavior in the society. But while governmental and university groups were tightening the noose of research findings, the industry was still insisting that the case was not yet proved. The public, meanwhile, felt something was terribly wrong, but lacked the organizational structure to do anything about the degree of violence, which continued to mount even while the controversy raged. Also, some vigilante groups, tired of promises and no action by the broadcasting industry, began to take matters into their own hands by initiating boycotts and urging the passage of censorship laws in communities and states.

The National Council of Churches decided it was imperative to do something about both the increase of violence and the increasing threats of censorship. But to take action, it first needed the facts. In 1983 its Communication Commission established a special study committee "to examine the problems of exploitative sex and gratuitous violence in the media." The purpose was to discover the extent and nature of violent and sexually violent material in the media, and what effects it is having on people in our society. One aim was to help church people and the public to identify the issues. A second was to identify solutions that would not place constraints on the rights of citizens to express themselves freely in a democracy.

The 10-member committee began with the assumption that the amount and the vicious character of violence coming into the home was steadily increasing. Whereas for many years, people who wished to see violent movies had to pay an entrance fee and enter a theatre, television sets now were making such material easily accessible in the home to children below the age of discretion. And with cable TV in almost half of American homes, and videocassettes expected to be in more than that number by 1987, violent programming was far more available than ever before.

The committee recognized that sexuality and violent action is found in all of life, and that the mass media would be dishonest if it were to attempt to "sanitize" this dimension of the human condition. For these reasons, the commission focused on "*exploitative* sex" and "*gratuitous* violence."

Also, the group was careful to recognize that the relationships between viewing violence and violent behavior do not operate in a social vacuum, and that many factors contribute to personal attitude and action, including a lack of parental supervision, inadequacies in our educational system, lack of adequate jobs for teenagers, lack of adequate social services, and the negative influences of peers. They assumed that the media are only one of many forces that shape our cultural environment, and that violence in the media is both a cause *and* an effect which reflects much that is wrong in society while at the same time amplifying some of its problems. As they stated in their final report: "The messages media carry help *create* our world, at the same moment that they reflect it. The choices made by writers, directors, producers, distributors and sponsors all contribute to what our world shall become" (p. 4).[13]

The study committee met eight times from mid-1983 to mid-1985. It held three public hearings, one focused on the research findings (in New York City), a second on the views of the communications industry (in Los Angeles), and a third on policy proposals and alternatives (in Washington, D.C.). It heard testimony from 31 persons, including researchers, producers, directors, writers, actors, corporate executives, legislators, and leaders of national educational and public interest organizations.

Research Findings

To get at the most recent facts about violence and the media, the committee consulted seven eminent researchers in the field. Dr. Edward Donnerstein of the Center for Communication Research at the University of Wisconsin told the hearing that his study of films which combine erotic material with violence indicates that exposure of young men to violent sexual scenes, especially rape, tends to desensitize them to aggression toward women. He emphasized that the negative influence is the element of *aggression,* not the *sexual* component. He and his coresearcher, Dr. Neil Malamuth, Chair of the Department of Communications at UCLA, believe that the increase in "slasher" films and R-rated violence movies in general ("I Was a Teenage Werewolf," "I Spit on Your Grave," "Maniac," "Texas Chainsaw Massacre," and "The Toolbox Murders") are creating a serious problem in homes where such films are now readily available via cable television and home video.

Dr. David Pearl, Chief of Behavioral Science, Department of Health and Human Services at the National Institute for Mental Health, had just conducted a 10-year follow-up study on behalf of the surgeon general's office.

Dr. Pearl said his study demonstrated that television has four effects on violent behavior:

(1) direct imitation of observed violence;

(2) "triggering" of violence which otherwise might be inhibited;

(3) desensitization to the occurrence of violence; and

(4) viewer fearfulness.

Regarding the overall social effect, Dr. Pearl warned:

> Consider the situation if even only one out of a thousand viewing children or youth were affected (there may well be a higher rate). A given prime-time national program whose audience includes millions of children and adolescents would generate a group of thousands of youngsters who were influenced in some way. Consider also the cumulative effects for viewers who watch such programs throughout the year. Even if only a small number of antisocial incidents were precipitated in any community, these often may be sufficient to be disruptive and to impair the quality of life for citizens of that community.[14]

Dr. George Gerbner, Dean of the Annenberg School of Communications at the University of Pennsylvania, released his 17th Violence Profile at the study committee's hearing on September 21, 1984. It indicated that the overall Violence Index in 1982–1983 once again had *not* diminished but was approximately at its 17-year average. However, violence in children's weekend programs reached a record *high*, with a rate of 30.3 violent incidents per hour against a 17-year average of 20.

> For the past 17 years, at least, our children grew up and we all lived with a steady diet of about 16 entertaining acts of violence (2 of them lethal) in prime time alone every night, and probably dozens if not hundreds more for our children every weekend. We have been immersed in a tide of violent representations that is historically unprecedented and shows no real sign of receding.[15]

Dr. Gerbner explained to the committee the role of television in creating a "mean and violent world" in the minds of many viewers—particularly heavy viewers:

> Humans threaten to hurt or kill, and actually do so, mostly to scare, terrorize, and impose their will upon others. Symbolic violence carries the same message. It is a show of force and demonstration of power. It is the quickest and most dramatic demonstration of who can get away with what against whom. . . .
>
> Violence as a scenario of social relationships reflects the structure of power in society and tends to cultivate acceptance of that structure. . . .

It is clear that women, young and old people, and some minorities rank as the most vulnerable to victimization on television. . . .

Most heavy viewers in every education, age, income, sex, newspaper reading, and neighborhood category express a greater sense of insecurity and apprehension than do light viewers. . . .

Fearful people are most dependent, more easily manipulated and controlled. . . . They may accept and even welcome repression if it promises to relieve their insecurities. That is the deeper problem of violence-laden television. [16]

Dr. Gerbner also charged that violence and sexual violence tend to vindicate existing inequities in the social order, especially to force "integration of the many into the prevailing hierarchy of powers." He called for mobilization of parents, educators, and religious and political leaders, not just to combat violence in the media, "but the larger structure of inequity and injustice behind it." [17]

He told the committee that he sees the structure of the industry and tax-exempt advertising—not censorship—as the barrier to a free market in television programming. "A handful of production companies create the bulk of the programs and sell them to broadcasters, not to viewers. The cheapest and least offensive programming is the most profitable," he says. Costs of such programming, like taxation, are borne by all, whether or not they use the products advertised, he points out, adding that the television "tax levy" on an average family in 1980 ranged from $80 in Atlanta to $29 in Wilkes-Barre—Scranton, Pennsylvania. "You pay when you wash, not when you watch," he told the committee. [18]

Dr. George Comstock, professor of communication at the Newhouse School of Communication, Syracuse University, has spent several years reviewing and analyzing all of the research having to do with violence and television from 1962 to the present. His statement to the NCC committee differed significantly from his statement of four years ago, quoted by CBS. Now, he testified: "A very large majority of studies report a positive association between exposure to media violence and aggressiveness." [19]

Dr. Comstock said that those surveys which reported statistically significant correlations typically associate "slightly less than 10% of the measured variance in aggression with exposure to television violence." He added that "given the presumably strong role of situational, long-term, environmental, social and personal factors that figure in behaving aggressively, it would be implausible to expect more than this clearly modest relationship."[20]

All but one of the other researchers substantiated the findings of Dr. Comstock. Dr. J. Ronald Milavsky, Director of Research for the National Broadcasting Company, concluded that the effects of viewing televised violence are too clouded by other factors to provide an unambiguous relationship to violent behavior:

> It has been my experience in studying mass communications effects that the more carefully done and the more realistic the study, the less likely one is to find effects. NBC has conducted several careful investigations of anti-social behavior which had such an outcome.[21]

With regard to his own research at NBC, Dr. Milavsky reported that "the study did not find evidence that television was causally implicated in the development of aggressive behavior patterns. In other words, watching programs with violence did not lead to increases in aggressive behavior either in the sample as a whole or in subgroups predisposed toward acting aggressively."[22]

Music video is a recent phenomenon which has become an influential factor in the lives of many children and teenagers. The committee heard testimony from Dr. Patricia Greenfield of UCLA that heavy viewing of music video may significantly increase violence in our society because it closely links erotic relationships with violence performed not by villains but by teenage idols. These programs, which combine the attraction of music, dancing, and exotic and creative backgrounds, become a powerful "selling" of violence, she said. The repetition of music videos, most of which are only 5 to 10 minutes in length, makes it possible for a teenager to see them dozens of times each week on cable. They also can be purchased as videocassettes. Repetitive viewing has an especially strong educative power, according to Dr. Greenfield.

The study committee concluded that violence in the media *does* lead to aggressive behavior by children, teenagers, and adults who watch the programs. This conclusion was based on laboratory experiments and field studies. The committee stressed that not all viewers become aggressive, of course, but the correlation between violence and aggressive behavior by some is undeniable. In the words of the committee: "Media violence is as strongly related to aggressive behavior as any other behavioral variable that has been measured. Further, certain types of media violence are increasing. Thus the research question has shifted from asking whether there is an effect from viewing violence to seeking explanations for the effects now demonstrated, and to identifying remedial actions."[23]

To help the general public understand the basic findings of the research, the study committee listed the following seven points:

1. Laboratory studies have shown conclusively that there is a causal relationship between viewing violence on television and subsequent aggressive behavior.

2. Although it is technically impossible to prove a cause-and-effect relationship in most field studies, the vast majority of such studies demonstrates a positive association between exposure to media violence and aggressiveness. (The committee believes that in the light of the evidence that does exist, for the media industry to demand absolute proof of such a relationship before action is taken is self-serving and unprincipled.)

3. The positive association between viewing TV violence and aggressiveness is on the order of a 10% variance in behavior. Looked at across the entire population and over a period of time, this modest statistical relationship implies a substantial negative social effect.

4. The conclusion that media violence encourages antisocial and aggressive behavior is consistent with accepted theories about the nature of social learning.

5. Violent sexual material stimulates aggression toward women and children. Also, violence stimulates sexual violence.

6. Because music video combines erotic material, teen idols, and violence in a repetitive context, this new format requires careful research and monitoring. Existing research on media violence in general implies a serious negative effect of violent and sexually violent music videos on children and young people.

7. Most children and adults who are heavy viewers of television express a greater sense of insecurity and apprehension about their world—the "mean world" syndrome—than do light viewers, and the generation of insecurity, vulnerability, and dependence creates the overall condition in which violence is facilitated in society.[24]

It is clear from this summary of the research that violence on television, as well as in the other media, is lowering our quality of life.

Whether or not we personally watch the excessive amounts of TV violence, enough people do see the violence so that there is more crime, more abuse, more injuries, and more deaths in our society than if we did not have the TV violence. People are suffering in the real world because we allow violence to persist in the world of television.

Of course, television can never be "sanitized" to the point that it contains no violence at all, nor should it. Such a depiction of life would be dishonest in a different way. The problem is *gratuitous* and *excessive* violence, which is sufficiently identifiable that society could correct the problem, if it had the will.

To repeat, television certainly is not *the* cause of violence in American society. Many other factors are involved, including individuals, the home, schools and churches, the work and recreation environments, and the society as a whole. But television has been identified, clearly and unambiguously, as *a* cause of violence, and television is something over which society has much more control than many of the other causes. It uses public airwaves which the Congress has said must be used for the public welfare. It comes into the home as a guest, rather than as a right of the broadcaster. It depends on public support, not only in our choosing to view but also in our choosing to buy the products which fund it. It is accorded special privilege in our society, and it must accept the special responsibilities which go with that privilege.

Some observers say we are faced with a mental pollution that is just as dangerous as our physical pollution. But how does a free society combat mental pollution? It is clear that some in the media industries hide behind the First Amendment. But at the other end of the spectrum lurk those true believers who are anxious to impose on the rest of us whatever version of morality is theirs. Somewhere between these polarities there must be a middle way which enables society to curb harmful violence without curbing freedom of speech.

The next question we face, therefore, is, Who is in charge? Who has the power to change the situation? And how does a free society make its will known about the fact that media violence is dangerous to our health?

NINE

WHAT WE CAN DO ABOUT MEDIA VIOLENCE[1]

The power that keeps cities of men together
Is noble preservation of law.

Euripides (421 B.C.)

It is not enough to show people how to live better;
there is a mandate for any group with enormous
powers of communication to show people how to *be*
better.

Marya Mannes, *But Will It Sell?* (1964)

Who's in Charge?

If media violence, and sexual violence in particular, in fact do threaten
the quality of American life, then how do the creative and managerial
people in television feel about the use of violence in their productions,
and what are the pressures within the industry that result in such a high
degree of violence? Who is responsible for the violence? Who makes
the decisions? The actors? Directors? Producers? Distributors? Networks? Sponsors? And what can concerned citizens do about the problem?

The NCC Study Committee discussed these issues with a number
of the creative people in Los Angeles, people who spend most of their
time bringing into being, in one way and another, the world of television. They found the responses disturbing, though perhaps predictable.

First, individual members of the industry *are* concerned, many of them profoundly, about the increasing amount of sex and violence in the media in which they work.

For example, from Christine Foster, a major TV producer: "Mainstream, legitimate network and production company executives, producers, writers and directors, are, like you, conscientious citizens, family people, mothers and fathers. . . We are conscious of the effect we have on the public and on our communities."[2]

From Robert E. Lee, writer of "Inherit the Wind" and "Auntie Mame": "The 'media' is a collection of very intelligent people in a very difficult situation. Most creative people are *not* exploitative; they are high minded."[3]

Second, the study committee discovered that the people working in the media industries are part of a vast and complex system which parcels out responsibility, a little bit to everyone, so that, in the end, *no one* is ultimately responsible. For example, when participants in the Los Angeles hearing were asked, "Who has the responsibility to do something about the problem of sex and violence?" the committee got answers which consistently placed responsibility on someone *else*.[4]

From Gene Reynolds (independent television producer-director): "We need to persuade the network executives to lead the way."

From David Soul (Hutch in "Starsky and Hutch"): "The actors are the most honest—and the least powerful—group in Hollywood."

From Maurie Goodman (head of NBC's Broadcast Standards in Hollywood): "The members of Broadcast Standards all want NBC to do *good* programming."

From Christine Foster (production house producer): "I think that the public is exposed to too much gratuitous violence and too much exploitative sex. I'm particularly concerned with the depiction of violence and disrespect against women. [But] studio executives are intelligent, brutally overworked men and women who share one thing in common with baseball managers: they wake up every morning of the world with the knowledge that sooner or later they're going to get fired. They report to Executive Vice Presidents, who report to Senior Vice Presidents, who report to Presidents, who report to Group Presidents, who report to the Chairman of the Board, who reports to the stockholders who report to the IRS, who, I guess, report to God."

And from Bill Sackheim (film and TV writer): "Ninety percent of the people in this business want to do good work. . . . . It is the audience who ultimately are the masters."

In summary, actors say they only do what they are told by the writers and directors; writers and directors say producers require them to put more sex and violence into the shows; producers say it is the networks that demand more sex and violence; networks say their choices are limited, the competition is brutal, and the sponsors demand results. Everyone agrees they don't like the amount of exploitative sex and gratuitous violence which they, together, create.

What about the sponsors? Gene Reynolds charged that "sponsors in the last twenty years have escaped responsibility." David Levy (President of the Caucus of Producers, Directors, and Writers) explained that some 20 years ago sponsors normally purchased a whole *series* of programs on television or radio—Kraft, Hallmark, Texaco, and so on—but that today sponsors only purchase *time*—a few minutes of spot advertising on many different programs. Thus the sponsors now reach many different audiences many times each day, but in doing so diffuse their responsibility for any particular program among a half-dozen or more other sponsors.

Sponsors clearly have an interest in the content of programs with which the public may associate their commercial message. For example, General Motors has had the following guideline for many years:

Our aim is to avoid association with those programs that appear to emphasize offensive subject matter and language for their own sake.[5]

Mr. George H. Pruette Jr. (Director of Public Affairs, Advertising, for General Motors) testified that "General Motors believes that positioning our advertisements in an environment of exploitative sex and gratuitous violence which violate the accepted standards of a community is not in the best interests of either the Corporation or to the sale of its products."

David Levy summed up the situation by saying that "there are no 'wild men' in the media today. Instead, they are all in a System that traps them."[6]

Third, each TV network has only one ultimate objective—to win the largest number of viewers during *every half hour of every day*. This ratings drive is the economic reality which in many ways lies at the root of the problem, at least in television.

David Levy, a former network executive, TV producer, and long-time observer of the media world, pointed out that two and three decades ago the networks found time for programs that were not sponsored at all but were provided, without charge, as a public service. Today this is no longer true, mainly because no network can afford to let the opposition get even slightly ahead in the ratings which determine the rates for hundreds of millions of dollars of advertising billings each year. To take a hypothetical example, if ABC and CBS can deliver 1000 viewers to an advertiser for $10, but NBC can deliver 1000 viewers for $9 then NBC is considered "number one"—and *all* the sponsors will rush to it to get the better buy for the season. As Christine Foster said, "Let's not kid ourselves, the network ratings race is business war." [7]

This business war results in what media consultant and former NBC executive Paul Klein called "the least objectionable programming"—a schedule designed *not* to reach diverse audiences at different times with programming of considerable interest to them, but instead designed to reach the *largest possible audience all the time*. The latter requires programming that is as *unobjectionable* (not as entertaining or as enlightening) to as many people as possible. This practice is what makes so much television programming look the same: it has to be the same, to deliver the largest possible audience—which is the "product" the networks sell to the sponsors—for the smallest amount of dollar per viewer.

Given this system, advertisers are held to be economically responsible when they buy the cheapest programs which reach the largest number of viewers with their message, regardless of quality. And so networks would be considered economically irresponsible by their stockholders if they did not provide the cheapest possible programs which would reach the largest possible audience, regardless of content, in order to make the largest number of sales and profits.

But why does this economic system drive the actors, writers, directors, and producers to create gratuitous sex and violence?

Said writer Robert Lee: "Is there too much violence on the airwaves, screens, stages of America? Of course there is. Why? It's easier. It takes less ingenuity to get and hold an audience by hitting people on the head with a baseball bat than with an idea."

And Steve Bello, staff writer on a current TV hit, agreed: "It requires more time, effort and creativity to write and produce a segment that involves the interaction of three different people, than to do an equal amount of time of a car chase or shoot-out."[8]

Cost savings, combined with what researcher Dr. Jerome Singer documents as the importance of *movement and action* as an immediate attention-getter, account for much of the pressure for gratuitous violence on the screens in our homes.

There are three major reasons for the high amount of sexual violence and overall violence in programs: (1) monopoly control of program production and distribution by a handful of powerful companies; (2) the drive for profits far in excess of those enjoyed by the vast majority of American corporate business, and (3) the failure of the Federal Communications Commission to exercise adequate oversight of broadcasting.

Sharon Maeda (public radio executive): "We need a change in the present rules governing the ownership of broadcast stations. There's too much monopoly."[9]

Robert Lee (playwright): "The airwaves are different from the theatre: they are yours and mine. The Broadcasting Act of 1934 was a Bill of Rights which requires responsibility. But we now have a third-rate lawyer as head of the FCC—a man who has done more to jettison the intent of the Act than anyone else."[10]

David Levy (Caucus of Producers, Directors, and Actors): "Today the FCC shows absolutely no responsibility whatever. Mr. Fowler [then Chairman of the FCC] should resign—a toothless tiger."[11]

Deregulation of broadcasting and the FCC's apparent indifference to the character and the practices of broadcast licensees and cable operators in effect seem to legitimize the operation of these media as businesses like any other business, disregarding the public trusteeship that is required by the Communications Act. In spite of the view of writer Bill Sackheim that "ninety percent of the people in this business want to do good work," the FCC has created a regulatory vacuum that inevitably fosters inexpensive, low-quality programming which, to be cheap and yet get instant mass attention, must become increasingly violent.

What can be done? The study committee concluded:

The current philosophy of the FCC and the industry that marketplace forces will guarantee the provision of quality programming that will satisfy the public interest is questioned by the creative elements in the industry, and by this Committee. There is widespread opinion that the guidance of programming should *not* be left to the interplay of market forces alone. The risks are too great to American families and to the functioning of our democratic system of government. In spite of industry claims to the contrary, the Committee found no indication that audience members have any say in what should be in programs or how programs should be distributed.[12]

Some Middle Axioms

Again, some middle axioms, between fundamental principles and day-by-day strategy, may prove helpful in considering what actions to take in responding to the problem of media violence:

1. All mass media are educational. Whether they deal with information, opinion, entertainment, escape, explicit behavior models, or subtle suggestion, the mass media always, directly or indirectly, shape values.

2. Only a genuinely open marketplace of ideas can guarantee the search for truth. The First Amendment must be defended because it guarantees freedom of religion, of speech, and of the press. Society should seek to maximize the diversity of sources and ideas, and to minimize the power of government or individuals to block or constrict this diversity of sources.

3. Prior control of the content of media does exist in our society—exercised by government, by business, by education, by the power of money and monopoly. With respect to any individual program, someone must decide what shall be included, or what is left out. The issue is not whether there should be prior control, but who should exercise it, and how it should be exercised.

4. Freedom must be exercised within a framework of responsibility.

5. The airwaves are held in trust for the public by radio and television broadcasters, and their licenses are regulated by government. While the broadcaster is therefore responsible for the content of programming, this right does not abridge the public's "right to know" and to be fairly represented on the air.

6. Television and cable deliver unsolicited images into homes and thus are different from media which are sought by users on their own initiative. The television and cable industries, especially because the

broadcast spectrum and wiring systems are limited, have a special responsibility to serve the public interest.

7. Industry self-regulation should be supported. But self-regulation can be only a partial solution, because without governmental regulation the industry's self-interest finally will take precedence over the public interest.

8. In any competitive business environment some rules are necessary to bring about positive change. Laws and governmental regulation are essential in dealing with reform in the communication industry because they can place all competitors on an equal basis and thus not disturb the working of the economic marketplace.

9. In all broadcast and film media, advance information about the products offered should be made available by the industry to parents to help them guide their children's viewing.

Policy Recommendations

In the light of these middle axioms, there are several actions which the public and the churches should consider to help alleviate the problems related to violence and sexual violence in television. Since so much "television" now is actually cable TV and videocassettes, these subsidiary media also require consideration. It is important to note that each of these three is subject to different regulations and therefore different solutions. While television stations are licensed by the FCC, cable systems receive local franchises for the right to string wires along city streets, and in this sense operate more like a telephone company than a television station. And videocassette stores are subject to zoning and other municipal laws regulating them as retail outlet stores.

Television

The key to solving the problems of violence on television is basically for broadcasters to exercise their responsibility to serve the public welfare. This will happen only when the Federal Communications Commission reasserts its oversight of the broadcasting industry on behalf of the public interest. Broadcasting was deregulated during the early 1980s, and as long as deregulation remains in effect, there is no way that the public can expect an industry that is engaged in a constant "business war" over ratings to take seriously its social obligation to reduce the amount of violence in its programming.

Broadcasting networks and stations should be required by the Federal Communications Commission to carry on all movies already rated by the Motion Picture Classification and Rating Administration the ratings now in use (G, PG, PG-13, R, and X), with additional short descriptive phrases that indicate the amount and intensity of violence in programs. Ratings and descriptions should appear in on-the-air promotions for programs, in newspaper and television guide listings, and in network, sponsor, and station advertisements.

The FCC should be required to conduct annual hearings, open to the public, in which producers of television programming (networks, stations, syndicators, production houses, sponsors) would be required to explain how and by whom decisions are made to determine the content of entertainment programs. Only by such public discussion can the present anonymity of program decision making be penetrated and responsibility for program content be fixed. Stations should also be required to meet regularly with members of the public to discuss and assess the content and effects of entertainment programs, and the relationships of these programs to generally accepted community mores. Participation in such consultations on the broadcasting side should require the presence of the highest-ranking decision makers of networks and stations.

Further actions can be taken regarding programming, without infringing on the First Amendment rights of broadcasters. Networks and stations could be required by law to devote a percentage of their air time, production budgets, and facilities to children's programming. This programming could be created and produced in cooperation with a broad spectrum of organizations and individuals with concern for children. In the case of local programming, a local Community Media Action Board could assist. Local groups could pool their production resources at the national level, thereby making possible nationally produced materials of high quality.

Television stations could be required by Act of Congress to provide regularly scheduled programming for children, Monday through Friday during after-school hours, at a time when older children could view it (4 P.M. to 6 P.M.). Tax incentives could be provided to producers of creative children's programming, just as such incentives now encourage urban housing, solar energy developments, educational organizations, and other areas which benefit the entire society.

Incidents of violence should not be included in commercial announcements, such as trailers that advertise violent movies. If violent commercials are run, then free counteradvertising time should be accorded to local community groups under the Fairness Doctrine. In the 1960s, when the FCC required stations to run counteradvertisements every time an ad for cigarettes was played, the broadcasting industry soon agreed to legislation prohibiting all smoking ads, since the alternative was to run one *free* minute for every paid minute of cigarette advertising. The same mechanism could work against violent commercials.

If local communities must take responsibility for that part of the education of their children which is occurring through television, local TV stations will pay attention. Traditionally, education has taken place in the public schools, and public school boards were set up in recognition of this fact. Members of the boards are elected to act on behalf of parents to oversee the process of education. But today children spend more hours watching television than they spend in school. Television has become the Great Teacher.

Therefore, what is now needed is some media-related equivalent of the local school board which can monitor the educational aspects of television in the community. One way to achieve this would be to establish local community Media Education Boards, which would not determine programs the stations would put on the air, but rather would assist radio and television stations in meeting the educational needs of the children in their community. Or, the local school board could regularly advise the local radio and TV stations regarding their educational obligations.

The National Education Association has announced plans to establish hundreds of local Teacher-Parent Partnerships which could form the basis of local monitoring groups to assess the effectiveness of radio and television stations in meeting the educational needs of their children. Other community groups, such as libraries, professional organizations, public health and safety agencies, the colleges and churches—all could contribute to helping local stations focus much more on their educational obligation to the community.

"Education" here is *not* restricted to "instruction." Broadcasting from its very beginnings has had broadly educational impact which has never been properly recognized, and broadly educational potential which it has never realized. However, the development of local community groups to monitor local station responsibilities for children will not work unless deregulation is reversed and the FCC once again asserts its role of insuring that broadcasters meet their public-service responsibilities.

Cable

Most distributors of films via satellite to cable systems (Home Box Office, Cinemax, Showtime, etc.) use the MPAA ratings. It would be a major step forward if the MPAA film-rating system were to be adopted by the cable industry. This step would involve a commitment on the part of all "member" cable companies to make the ratings available in all advance information, schedules, and promotion as well as on the screen at the time of showing, as recommended for television broadcasting stations.

In addition, under the Cable Communications Policy Act, cable operators are now required to make available by lease or sale a lockbox device which allows the subscriber to use a key to lock out the viewing of a particular cable service. However, the lockbox is not required as part of the basic channel selector supplied by the cable company. Since parents are required to make special provisions to get the lockbox feature, very few are actually in use. An even more significant step would be for the Congress to require all cable companies to make the lockout feature available on all channel switching devices it normally provides to its subscribers. The lockout makes one or more channels temporarily unavailable.

In addition, cable companies should be required to place all R- and X-rated films on a channel separate from other movies. For example, HBO, Cinemax, and The Movie Channel each would be required to have an "A" channel for family fare and a "B" channel for the more violent and sexually explicit films. This division would allow parents easily to lock out films deemed objectionable for their children, and still have access to them when desired. Suppliers such as Disney, which run only G, PG, or PG-13 films would still have only a single channel, as would Playboy and other suppliers of exclusively R- and X-rated films. The advantage of this plan is that it does not restrict access on the part of adults while it gives parents more freedom of choice about what their children can see at home.

Videocassettes

The number of stores renting and selling videocassettes has increased dramatically during the past decade. Fifty percent of homes now have VCRs, and this number is expected to increase steadily. The *New York Times* reports that dealers estimate that between 20% and 40% of cassettes rented in videostores are in the category of sexually explicit material. Virtually all of the R and PG-13 films which contain violent and sexually violent material are available for sale in videocassette stores.

But videocassettes do not come into the home by the turn of a switch. In this sense they are more like books or magazines than television, and they are entitled to the same First Amendment protection that is accorded to books and magazines. On the other hand, videocassettes must be rented or purchased in retail stores in the local community, and are subject to the same municipal laws as other retail outlets. Therefore, the only action which is consistent with free expression, no matter how much some individuals may dislike the content of the videocassette, is to require that videos intended for adults (R-rated, X-rated, and unrated) not be displayed prominently in storefronts and not sold or rented to persons under 17 years of age.

The First Amendment does not extend its protection of speech to children. The Supreme Court has taken the position that society has the obligation to make a judgment as to what speech is appropriate for children, just as persons under a certain age are not allowed to drink, drive, or vote. Thus, the sale to children of videocassettes which the society decides are inappropriate for them can be prohibited. However, to take more restrictive legal action with regard to adults would unduly restrict their First Amendment rights. To allow government the authority to decide what adults may see and hear represents a greater threat to the welfare of the society than to allow expressions which may be objectionable to some.

The Public

There are several positive things which individuals and groups can do to deal with the problem of violence. First, community and church groups should *encourage excellence*.

At the NCC Study Committee hearing in Los Angeles, Gene Reynolds, the producer and writer of "M*A*S*H," pointed out that the

Humanitas Awards of the Paulists have had considerable positive effect on writers and producers in the industry. The Humanitas Award provides $10,000 for the best program each year that stresses ethical principles and eschews gratuitous violence. For more than two decades the National Council of Churches has presented annual awards to films which "illumine the human condition." Clearly, the church and public, both nationally and—perhaps even more importantly—locally, could do much more to recognize and to encourage creative writers, directors, producers, sponsors, station performers, managers, and owners who strive to provide programs that uplift ethical values and humane relationships in their programming.

Another public strategy which holds great promise for affecting the directions the media take on violence, is *corporate stockholder action.* Holders of stock in companies which advertise on television or cable can call the attention of the officers and directors to the importance of adopting voluntary guidelines which would forbid sponsorship of programs with exploitative sex and gratuitous violence. This approach has been used by a number of public-interest groups, including churches, and has been found to be effective. However, far more attention by sponsors will be needed before reaching the "threshold point" which would send a clear signal to the industry that less violence is demanded. Such an approach should be given a high priority by public-interest groups and churches, since it is equitable, clear, and manageable.

A more drastic action is to initiate a *petition to deny license renewal.* Deregulation of radio and television by the FCC does not change the provisions of the Communications Act. Whether or not the FCC checks on the performance, stations are still required "to broadcast in the public interest. . ." and to prove at renewal time that they have exercised responsible trusteeship in exchange for their licenses. In communities where there is dissatisfaction with the performance of one or more stations, public groups may legally file petitions with the FCC to deny license renewals. The current FCC majority may reject such petitions, but the petitioners have standing to challenge an FCC decision in the U.S. Circuit Court of Appeals, where adherence to the law may be expected. However, it requires considerable money, expertise, and time to be successful in such litigation. The cases which the national church organizations won during the 1960s and 1970s took 5 to 15 *years* to complete.

A final word must be said about consumer boycott. Customer protest in front of stations, theaters, or stores is entirely constitutional and is a part of the American way of life. So is the withholding of purchases from a store, theater, or product. Boycotts have been attempted against major sponsors and television networks, but without any long-lasting effect.

While boycott is a legal and sometimes effective tool in situations where litigation and other recourses have been exhausted, it also is a very blunt tool which easily gets out of control and can hurt innocent people. For example, the boycott of a particular national food supplier could have ripple effects which would hurt grocers, truck drivers, and even farmers. Boycotts therefore should be used only as a last resort, only after all legal remedies have been exhausted, and then with great restraint.

Conclusions

We have suggested several ways to help the people in the creative and dynamic television industry to "do good work"—to produce programs which entertain and delight millions but do so without the exploitative sex and gratuitous violence which clearly result in real-life violence and consequent damage to the quality of life for millions of people in our nation. The First Amendment guarantees the freedom to speak whatever we wish, since one person's heresy is another person's truth. But the media industries hide behind this freedom, to the injury of all. Deciding where the middle way lies, which enables society to curb harmful violence without curbing freedom of speech, is difficult, and it will require us to consider what kind of society we really want.

Clearly, violence and sexual violence in the media must be reduced. The important thing to stress is that this goal can be attained without depriving those in the media of the means of livelihood or of the rewards which are justly theirs, and without depriving citizens of their First Amendment guarantee of freedom of speech. It will require concerned citizens to understand the extent to which the whole *system* of commercial broadcasting in America establishes an environment encouraging, not violent programming itself, but the conditions which result in violent programming. Profits require large audiences and economies of production. Large audiences require vivid, exciting, simple movement. Economies of production require stereotypes and action rather than complex relationships. Sponsors want audiences, networks engage in "business war," and writers and directors get the message: more violent action.

In one sense no one is in charge, hence no one can be blamed. But in another sense, everyone must share the blame—including the audience, the industry, and the political leaders who symbolically wash their hands of the problem by leaving it to "the marketplace." So long as we allow television to be an instrument for sales rather than for communication, the situation will persist, regardless of the number of statements viewing with alarm, or quality of the leaders deploring the situation, or the extent of boycotts of a network or station or program. In fact, such tactics as these often do more harm than good, since they tend to draw off much of the rightful righteous indignation of community leaders into rhetoric with no real results.

The solution may require that the situation get even worse before citizens will act. The danger then is that the movement will be toward censorship rather than toward changing the system. It is to be hoped that, instead, cooler heads will prevail and that citizens, through their elected leaders, will create by law the incentives which will encourage the industry to reduce the violence while still making a good living. A single law requiring children's programming in every community would be a good start. Expecting the FCC to regulate in the name of the citizens rather than the broadcasting industry would be another.

But this will take time, education, and community action. And it will require exploring in considerably more depth another closely related issue—the conflict between censorship and regulation of television.

TEN

HOW TO BUST
THE COMMUNICATION
TRUST

Congress shall make no law respecting an
establishment of religion, or prohibiting the exercise
thereof; or abridging the freedom of speech, or of the
press; or the right of the people peaceably to
assemble.

First Amendment, U.S. Constitution

Without a free press there can be no free society.
Freedom of the press, however, is not an end in itself
but a means to the end of a free society.

Justice Felix Frankfurter (1946)

I have never met a person who favors censorship. Everyone is opposed
to censorship. . . BUT. What follows the "but" tells us what forms
of censorship a person supports, for just as almost no one favors censorship, almost no one favors *absolute* free speech.

It is important to sort out the issues involved in freedom of speech
and the First Amendment (for these are two different things), and to
develop some principles and some strategies for keeping the media of
communication open and free as best suits an open and free democracy.
To do this we need first to look at some of the misunderstandings about
censorship.

Censorship Misunderstood

The first misunderstanding many people have is that the First Amendment protection of free speech, namely, that "Congress shall make no law abridging the freedom of the press or of speech," is absolute. But only a fanatic can seriously hold that the use of words should always be acceptable in society, regardless of any of its consequences. Legally, and I think also morally, freedom of speech in America does not include the right to utter slander, to publish libel, to cry "Fire!" in a crowded theater, to incite to riot, to perjure oneself, to advertise falsely, to conspire to overthrow the government, to use someone else's copyright, to utter speech which is in contempt of court, or to advocate a particular religious doctrine in the public schools. After living almost 200 years under the First Amendment, we have laws which either punish or prevent the freedom of all of these forms of speech.

Morally, we know that we must constantly choose between conflicting evils and conflicting goods in this world, that we sometimes have to sacrifice the beautiful in the interest of the good or true, or truth in the interest of kindness, or happiness and security in the interest of justice. The real question, then, is: *To what extent are we willing to give up the value of absolute freedom of expression in order to protect society from expressions which might destroy other values in our society, or the society itself?*

A second misunderstanding is that there is at present no censorship in the mass media. In fact, all mass communication media are subject to censorship, not in the sense of prior restraint by government, but in the sense of prior restraint by industry. Television network "program acceptance" departments "clear" every controversial word, action, and subject, and advertising agencies and sponsors exert powerful constraints on what is permitted to be said and seen. To be sure, private censorship is preferable to governmental censorship. But to what extent should censorship of either be tolerated in a democracy?

A third misunderstanding is that television "gives the people what they want." We have shown that what television really provides is the least offensive program to the most people possible, at all times. Television does not attempt to provide a variety of programs for a variety of audiences, so that a mix of programs over a period of several hours would provide what many different "audiences" want. Rather it attempts to reach as many different people as possible *all at once*. The reason is that television is not used in America to inform or even to entertain, but to deliver an audience to sponsors who can sell them products. The individual viewer has only the option of choosing the least-objectionable program or of pressing the "off" button, which cuts that part of the public off from the communication system—a system designed to meet the needs of business rather than the needs of the public.

The Limits of Freedom

In American television, a small minority, in the interest of profit, exercises control and effective censorship over a medium which is protected by a governmental guaranteed monopoly but which, in the name of freedom of speech, the government itself cannot control.

To understand how this came about, we have to go back to the founding fathers and to John Stuart Mill. Mill said that every individual has an absolute right to live as he pleases, up to the point where his conduct violates the rights of others. Within that sphere of liberty the individual has the freedom to express any opinion, to develop any tastes, to live life in his own way—a political philosophy which found its way, through Jefferson and others, into our Constitution and Bill of Rights.

With Mill's political philosophy came Adam Smith and his *Wealth of Nations,* which became the theoretical basis for our economic way of life. The concept of capitalism held that the best interests of all would be served if every person sought his own economic good. Competition would bring about efficiency and quality, and the true needs of the marketplace would be met.

But we soon learned that the marketplace economy did not work this way. It did not operate automatically to bring about efficiency and quality. Instead, large and powerful producers tended to get larger and more powerful until finally they monopolized parts of the marketplace. Then, instead of increasing quality, they increased profits. The needs of the marketplace were superseded by the power of monopoly. Instead of true choice increasing, it diminished. Instead of costs going down, they went up. Men such as Andrew Carnegie and John D. Rockefeller got richer and richer, and the commonwealth—that is, the welfare of the average citizen—suffered. When this happened, people realized that they needed a countervailing power to keep competition open—

to establish a true economic marketplace once again. And so citizens, through their elected representatives, created antitrust laws and set up regulatory agencies to make up for the deficiencies in Mill's philosophy and Adam Smith's economics.

Now we are beginning to realize that this same flaw is at work in the marketplace of communication. The power bases of communication—the publishers, broadcasters, cable companies, and so on—are tending to become so centralized and so powerful that genuine competition of ideas is being suppressed. The best ideas do not necessarily win out. Indeed, many alternative ideas are not effectively communicated at all. Instead, the communication monopolies tend to restrict the output of those ideas and assumptions that challenge or even question their own values and assumptions. They tend to present only the information and ideas that benefit them most. As a result, the welfare of the average citizens, in sense of their ability to know enough about their society to make wise decisions, begins to deteriorate. Their First Amendment rights are violated de facto.

As the large communications empires become more centralized and more powerful, they also become more self-serving, until today—as with the great iron and steel and railway and oil trusts in the 1890s—they threaten the welfare of the entire society. And, like those earlier trusts, while the efficiency of the communications empires goes up, competition goes down. The owners and operators function more and more in their private, rather than the public, interest. This leads to the conclusion that *something like antitrust laws in communication are necessary today to open up the marketplace of ideas.*

How did the nation get into a situation where its television is dominated by commercial interests whose primary objective is to deliver the audience to sponsors? The networks are by far the wealthiest part of this extremely wealthy industry. For more than 25 years, commercial television operations have returned a profit of 50-70% on tangible investments each year, as compared to a 20% return by most manufacturing concerns and roughly 10% for all U.S. industries.[1] One of the reasons for this unusual profitability is that the broadcasters are subsidized in several ways. First, the tax laws allow advertisers to write off advertising as a business expense, which reduces the cost to sponsors considerably. Second, the broadcasting industry is indirectly supported by the money the audience pays each year for the cost of sets (approximately $3 billion each year), and the cost of electricity to run them (which runs about another $1 billion).[2] Third, the way the electromagnetic spectrum was carved up guaranteed that every station would have very few competitors.

Also, the dominance of the three networks, and only three, was assured by the Federal Communications Commission when it decided to allocate television stations according to a fixed plan, rather than on a demand basis, and to allocate only three VHF stations in most middle-sized markets. The FCC then reserved a large amount of the remaining VHF spectrum for educational TV, thus further reducing the likelihood of competition. Roland Cass, a broadcast law expert, finds that "the VHF allocation pattern virtually guaranteed the viability of three, and only three, networks, and at the same time it provided the means for networks to capture a large share of the profits earned jointly by them and their affiliates."[3]

The three-network domination has clear effects on programming. Since advertisers want to support only the lowest possible price per viewer reached, and since there are only three networks, any one of the commercial networks will refuse to continue to air a prime-time series viewed in fewer than 15 million homes, and 20 million (still less than one-third of the total viewers each night) is not considered a real success. Furthermore, the degree or intensity of viewer interest in a given program is *irrelevant,* since advertising dollars depend almost completely upon the number of viewers, not the viewers' interest in the message or program. Thus there is a built-in bias in the system toward the production of the lowest-cost program that is the *least objectionable* to the largest number of people—which is the very opposite of the idea that competition will force better-quality programs.

However, if the bulk of the national TV audience were divided six ways instead of three, which is both technically and economically possible, a network would be encouraged to show at least some programming that was the first choice of a sixth of the population, even if the other five-sixths would rate it well down in their ranking of viewing options. And if there were 12 national sources of programming, even smaller audience-interest programming would be economically possible. The commercial nature of broadcasting would not be changed, but the number and variety of attractive program choices would increase dramatically.[4]

But the FCC has maintained the three-network system, which benefits the wealthiest and most powerful section of the broadcasting industry. In addition, for years the FCC crippled broadcasting's potential
rival, cable TV. In 1959, when cable was small and vulnerable, the
FCC insisted that it lacked authority to regulate it. But when cable
finally grew to become a threat to broadcasters, the FCC found that it
had authority, and it asserted that authority to hinder the growth of
cable-TV; among other restrictions, it required cable to carry local on-
air broadcasting and prohibited it from importing distant stations which
would provide competition to stations (and diversity for the audience).
Regarding the FCC's many subsequent rulings on cable, Cass writes
". . . it is plain that each of them serves the interests of TV broadcasters—each of the regulations either raises the cost of providing cable
services or reduces the attractiveness of cable programming."[5]

And, since 1980, the FCC has gone farther than ever before in
allowing the broadcast industry to establish a monopoly over the flow
of entertainment, news, and information to the American public.
Through a series of rulings, the FCC has deregulated broadcasting to
such an extent that the broadcaster has virtually no accountability for
the license which provides such enormous profits.

Deregulation has resulted in the creation of even larger communications conglomerates. For example, by abolishing its former rule that
a single company could own no more than seven TV stations, the FCC
set the stage for Capital Cities, already one of the largest "group"
owners of stations, to buy ABC, and for General Electric to buy RCA-
NBC. And by removing the requirement that a broadcaster must hold
a station at least three years before selling it, the FCC has encouraged
enormous trafficking in stations—the buying and selling of stations
like real estate. In late 1986, the FCC preapproved the sale of 160
stations, in some cases even *before the applications were completed,*
in order to allow broadcasters to benefit from the sales of stations before
the tax laws changed.

The deregulation of broadcasting is pernicious. It strikes at the heart
of the democratic ideals of wide-ranging and robust discussion, of
protection of the rights of minority views, of a genuine freedom of
information. What can the average citizen do to insist on public responsibility of those in positions of power in television?

Three Strategies to Keep Media Open

How do you bust a communication trust? The Bill of Rights does not forbid the Congress from making laws abridging the freedom to make *money,* and so Congress passed the Sherman Anti-Trust Act. But the Bill of Rights does forbid Congress from restricting speech, because, in a democracy, ideas—no matter how repugnant or revolutionary—must be capable of being heard and considered. Restriction of an idea is the first step toward thought control and totalitarianism. If government had been able constitutionally to restrict the press, the history of Vietnam and Watergate, for example, would have been entirely different, and today we might be enjoying far less freedom and democratic participation than we do.

But if governmental censorship for adults is to be avoided, and if private censorship (self-regulation) tends to be self-serving and repressive in another way, then how can members of the public express their views and work their will about the kind of society the mass media are cultivating? If the world of television is having a profound effect on the kind of real world we are living in, then the question is, Can television become more responsive to the need for citizens to determine who they are, what values they wish to support, and what kind of society they wish to live in?

There are three approaches which get at this problem, and they can do so without endangering First Amendment guarantees of free speech.

Political Action

The first approach is *direct political action.* This entails expecting and demanding that the existing regulatory processes work to protect the public rather than the industry they are supposed to regulate. The Federal Communication Commission has *never,* on its own initiative, withdrawn the license of a single television station. A few times when licenses have been withdrawn, the FCC has been *ordered* to do so by the courts, in effect, over the protests of the FCC itself. Congress keeps the commission's budget pitifully small—about the size of Anacin's annual advertising budget. And over the years, many administrations have added to the problem by making certain that FCC appointees were not found "objectionable" to industry leaders.

The result is that the American system of broadcasting has become, in the words of media historian Eric Barnouw, "an extraordinary example of governmental laissez-faire. It has allowed private companies, almost without restraints, to set up toll gates across public highways of communication and to exact a toll from the public. . . . Meanwhile the tolls, levied substantially on a what-the-traffic-will-bear basis, have tended to eliminate some elements of society from the marketplace of ideas and to give dominance to others."[6]

If the situation is so blatantly unjust, why doesn't the Congress unleash the FCC? Why can't the members of Congress just give the FCC enough money to do the job and insist on independent appointees from the president? The answer lies in a simple political fact of life: *all members of Congress depend on their local radio and television stations to get elected.* Those stations represent the most vital linkage they have to their constituents. The stations provide the positive image and the news and information that add up to crucial votes in every election.

More than the franking privilege, more than local newspapers, more than any other single medium, television is the politician's life-blood. At present there is nothing but goodwill that gets the incumbent broadcasting time. There is no law which says broadcasters must provide time between elections for those in office to report to their constituencies. Who can afford to bite the hand that feeds the voters? And so each time a bill comes up that would strengthen the FCC, all members of Congress are made acutely aware that a vote against the interests of the broadcasters back home could cost them vital exposure that keeps them in office.

This, then, is the Gordian knot of broadcast regulation. If a way can be discovered to require stations to provide time regularly to members of Congress, on the basis that it is the *right* of all citizens to have an opportunity to see and hear their chosen representatives, and if a similar requirement were to insure free access to all congressional candidates during elections—only then can the knot be severed. The results would be messy, and a good deal of boring TV undoubtedly would result. But the First Amendment would be implemented, not violated, by such a requirement, and one of the prices of citizenship may just be that we have to give up a few hours of entertainment each year in order to make representative government work.

Economic Pressure

The second approach is *economic pressure* to make communication more open and responsive to citizens' needs. But if political action requires the strength of Samson, then economic pressures require the wisdom of Solomon. How can one exert economic pressure against a repressive system without becoming repressive itself? Consumer education is less subject to abuse, but it is also slow and expensive. Media education is just beginning to take hold in the public schools and is almost altogether missing in the churches. Yet teaching people how to understand what the media are doing to them and helping them learn the techniques of media discrimination so that they can develop values and opinions and points of view which are their own could scarcely be more important to educators and church leaders.

But what is also required is countervailing power, and here the moral dilemmas emerge. Surely some kind of concerted citizen action is valid. Action for Children's Television (ACT), which grew out of the moral outrage of a few mothers in Boston to become a nationwide movement, performs an important public service. It organized protests against TV advertising of high-sugar foods to children. It cooperated with members of Congress to get support for bills to require one hour of children's programming daily during children's prime viewing time. It evaluates children's programming and provides this information to parents. It deserves continued support.

There are also economic strategies that have had various degrees of success. Church-related groups have organized stockholder action among corporations that advertise on high-violence programs. In one campaign, a dozen major advertisers agreed to avoid sponsoring ads on high-violence programs. The irony of this modest success is that in response to the pressure against violence the industry began to increase the amount of sexual titillation to compensate for turning down the violence.

Another example of the unpredictable outcome of citizen economic action is the boycott which Dr. Bob Jones III of Bob Jones University waged against General Motors Corporation for its sponsorship of "Jesus of Nazareth," the Zeffirelli biblical epic on the NBC network. Jones proclaimed it was un-Christian since it did not portray a literal version of the biblical events, and his threat to boycott GM cars so upset GM management that they pulled their advertisements and sponsorship two weeks before air time. But Proctor and Gamble, the largest sponsor of them all, saw the opportunity and bought up all of the spots for the series. The religious controversy merely provided NBC invaluable free advertising, and the series attracted one of the largest audiences in TV history. The program series has since been aired almost every year, and remains one of the better Bible epics. So much for boycott!

It is possible to draw some guidelines as to what is and is not a morally acceptable expression of the public will and the use of countervailing force with the communication industry. For example, in the case of the Action for Children's Television call for a ban on commercials for children too young to discriminate, or the church's protest against excessive and gratuitous violence, the criticism was aimed at a *class of programming* rather than against an individual program. In addition, the objections are not to an idea presented on a particular program, but against the *overall quality* or approach—in one case exploitation of children, in the other gratuitous violence. Finally, the objections are based on *careful research* developed by responsible experts and widely accepted by the public, in one case that children's ads exploit children who are not yet old enough to discriminate, and in the other that violence on television causes violence in actual behavior.

There are other moral distinctions. In the case of ACT and the churches, the approach to the communications industry has been through a combination of education, public protest, and stockholder action. Bob Jones, on the other hand, proposed boycott as the immediate and first step, and from a position of moral certitude which was presumptuous, vain, and intimidating, especially to Christians. Said Dr. Bob: "Those who love and know the Lord Jesus Christ, God incarnate, as their personal Lord and Saviour will, I am sure, make their protest known both verbally and by spending their automobile dollars elsewhere."[7]

Another example of the vagaries of boycott is the campaign waged against 7-Eleven Stores by the Rev. Donald Wildmon and his organization, in an attempt to get the chain to remove *Playboy* and *Penthouse* magazines from their shelves. At first the boycott seemed successful, in part because the Attorney General's Report on Pornography had listed the stores as "selling pornography." However, nearby stores reported that their sales of these two magazines soared, which means that while *Playboy* and *Penthouse* suffered slightly or perhaps not at all in the long run (because of the free publicity), the individual 7-Eleven owner-franchisers suffered considerable economic damage not only from the loss of magazine sales but from losses of additional sales from people who went to other stores to purchase *Playboy* and *Penthouse*. The Rev. Mr. Wildmon claimed a great victory, while both magazines continued to sell to those who wanted them.

On the other hand, Cesar Chavez vividly demonstrated that boycott can be used as a successful tool for redressing grievance. He used it in the case of the California grape-pickers' boycott as a last resort, after every other approach, including recourse to the courts, had failed. Still, boycott is a very blunt tool which inevitably hurts many innocent people in the process of hurting the targeted adversary. It should be used only after every other avenue has been exhausted, and then only with considerable precision and care, since unforseen results are likely.

Given the fact that there is no genuine "box office" for television, stockholder action probably represents one of the better approaches for making the will of the consumer known. But there can be unforseen results here as well. In an attempt to be as inoffensive as possible, sponsors may become reluctant to support *any* program with bite and controversy, with the result that TV may become even more devoid of serious content. This is another of the many ironies facing those who attempt to use economic sanctions to improve the openness of communication.

New Possibilities

The third general approach to media reform is a time-honored solution to repression of all kinds: *create new possibilities*. While we need to deal with the political givens, we need also to redefine those givens and to find those "zones of freedom" where we can help ourselves and others to see things differently.

One of the most significant creative alternatives to commercial broadcasting is public broadcasting. The Corporation for Public Broadcasting was created by Congress in 1967 to promote the development of the nation's noncommercial broadcast stations. The CPB budget grew steadily from $3 million in 1968 to $35 million in 1972. In 1969 the CPB set up the Public Broadcasting Service, which soon became a cooperative of member stations and the heart of a fourth network. In 1972, with "Sesame Street" leading the way, public broadcasting was beginning to gather a significant audience, and from then until 1980, federal funding for public broadcasting system steadily increased.

However, in 1980, the situation changed dramatically. The new Reagan Administration vowed to reduce federal funding for public broadcasting, and, by 1984, after a series of presidential vetoes, funding had been *cut* by 40% below the 1981 level. To stay on the air, public broadcasting stations were forced to resort to year-round fund-raising campaigns, to accept forms of "underwriter recognition" that looked suspiciously like commercials, and to tailor their programming schedule to whatever corporate underwriters would support.

We are the only nation in the Western world which takes the importance of public broadcasting so lightly. The entire income from all sources for the public radio and television system is about a half-billion dollars a year, or about one-half of what we spend on dog food.[8] Where are our priorities? Do we really care more about our dogs than our children?

In addition, National Public Radio is one of our national treasures, providing the only quality radio program for children on a daily basis, and airing every afternoon what is considered by news professionals to be the best radio news program in the world today, "All Things Considered." NPR is equally endangered by the current administration's hostility and lack of support. It deserves concerted action on the part of local groups to help fund their local NPR stations, and by national groups to insist that Congress increase the level of federal funding.

These "zones of freedom" can be found in curious places. For example, when "Sixty Minutes" originally went on the air, it was treated by management as a showcase for the News Division and was not expected to pull a substantial audience. Instead, "Sixty Minutes" eventually developed a large audience right in the middle of Sunday prime-time, a time, most of the industry thought, when people would opt for pure entertainment. When President Carter said he wanted to try to continue communicating with ordinary people, and seemed to mean it, Richard Salant, President of CBS News, suggested a radio call-in program. The result was "Ask President Carter," which had millions of listeners, and thousands of telephone calls—a new possibility in mass communication. Ronald Reagan continued the weekly radio program, but without the call-in feature that made it unique.

Some new possibilities occur simply by accident. Perhaps the most significant thing about the gavel-to-gavel coverage of the Watergate hearings by public broadcasting was not that it brought the scandal into so many homes, but rather that it gave many people a new *vision* of what television really could do for them and their nation. They realized, perhaps for the first time, that there is no reason why television has to supply only soaps by day and sitcoms and violence by night. Another vision of TV's possibilities occurred when PBS began to telecast great movies, *uninterrupted,* and people began asking why movies on commercial TV have to be halted every 10 minutes by jarring commercials. The response by the broadcasters is that "someone has to pay for the shows," but this distinctly lacks imagination. In England and Europe the commercials come in bunches, several minutes at a time, at the end of programs and, in some countries, only once an evening. Their commercials sell and broadcasters still make a profit.

Another zone of creative new possibility is community radio. These are usually small stations which put on the air what the larger commercial stations would not dare, with the result that they garner a small but significant audience of people who are willing to pay (through "listener subscriptions") for the privilege of not having their radio horizons hemmed in by talk-rock-news and top-40 music. Community radio also deserves stronger local support. And the potential for cable TV, low-power television, point-to-point TV, and other "narrowcast" innovations as creative alternatives to commercial broadcasting have been discussed in Chapter 7.

Organizing for Media Reform

The three strategies discussed above—political action, economic sanctions, and the creation of new possibilities—all depend on organized citizen action. But, during the first years of television, organized groups could scarcely expect to achieve any results at all, because the Federal Communications Commission refused to recognize representatives of the public as "parties of interest" in license proceedings. It was only in 1966, in response to litigation brought against the FCC by the United Church of Christ, that the D.C. Circuit Court of Appeals told the FCC it was required to permit citizens to participate in its business! This single ruling set the stage for the development of not only the broadcast reform movement, but the involvement of all other citizen action groups in other governmental agencies as well.

The reform groups that developed after 1966 were both many and varied. Most represented minorities which felt excluded from television: the Gray Panther Media Task Force, the National Organization for Women, the National Black Media Coalition, Action for Children's Television. Some, such as the Committee on Open Media, sought access for all under-represented groups, and a few, such as the Citizens Communications Law Center, offered *pro bono* legal assistance. The church-related groups supported a number of justice-related issues, and chief among the groups were the Office of Communication of the United Church of Christ, the Communication Commission of the National Council of Churches, the United States Catholic Conference, and the Inter-religious Committee for Corporate Responsibility. From 1969 until 1977 many of these groups found themselves members of the Advisory Committee of National Organizations (ACNO) of the Corporation for Public Broadcasting, and ACNO served as a forum and a stimulus for their activities. They were in constant contact with the FCC, the courts, the Congress, corporations interested in media reform, the Corporation for Public Broadcasting, and the public.

The list of accomplishments achieved by these reform groups during the period 1966 to 1980 is impressive. The right of the public to participate in regulation of the broadcasting industry was affirmed. Attempts by the broadcasters to reduce their public service obligations were beaten back. Presidential debates, increased public affairs, innovations in news coverage, fewer commercials on children's programs, more female and minority on-air employment, greater minority ownership of stations, "free speech messages" in many cities, greater responsiveness to viewer's letters, and a temporary reduction in violent programs—all were brought about through the efforts of the broadcast reform groups.[9] Unfortunately, virtually every one of these progressive steps has been reversed since 1980, when deregulation began. Since then, many of the reform groups have disbanded, unable to attract support because they could no longer get a hearing in Congress, the FCC, or the White House.

What are the possibilities for broadcast reform in the future? Fortunately, politics tends to move in cycles, and the growing public disaffection with the commercialization of television and radio is bound to be heard eventually in Washington. Given a political environment that is not actively hostile, the reform movement can be regenerated, but to do so it will need to take a somewhat different shape.

An analysis of the broadcast reform movement shows that concensus regarding *content* among the various groups was impossible; each minority was motivated primarily to get its own message across. Only the church organizations and legal aid groups were interested more generally in achieving a free marketplace of ideas. Furthermore, the smaller, more ad hoc groups not affiliated with established institutions had to indulge in grandstand plays in order to attract volunteers and money. And when ACNO dissolved, the groups lacked any opportunity to exchange ideas and learn from each other's experience.

An effective broadcast reform movement in the future will need a number of member groups which are affiliated with large, national organizations. It will have to attract a large public base which can be both a base of financial support and a channel for citizen education. Finally, it will require some central organization which can be flexible enough to involve groups with different agendas but strong enough to provide them with resources and a forum for the exchange and coordination of ideas and plans.

The central thrusts of a reborn reform movement should be stockholder action to effect corporate decision making, the mobilization of public influence on Congress, the development of improved rating systems, the encouragement of research to support policy-making, and the creation of support mechanisms to encourage and inform creative people working in the media industries.[10]

Conclusions

One of the enduring problems of society is that our social engineering lags behind our technical engineering, with the result that large commercial power bases tend to take over and dominate those parts of the new technology that increase their power and profits. Unfortunately, the public usually never knows what it has missed until it is far too late to create the laws and regulations that would allow the new technology also to benefit the public welfare.

There will be no remedial action to counter the overdose of violence on TV, nor will there be a thorough airing of matters of public importance, or the opportunity for the public to hear "fringe" positions, or quality programming for children, so long as the television industry is able to neutralize regulation through its power over members of Congress, and at the same time can forestall the development of economic countervailing forces by invoking the shibboleths of freedom, censorship, and the First Amendment. Freedom without responsibility is the freedom of the "free fox in the free henhouse" and leads to domination and repression that can be more dangerous in a democracy than the governmental regulation of licenses to insure the responsible use of a valuable public resource.

What is needed certainly is *not* governmental censorship. What is needed is a freeing up of the existing regulatory system so that broadcasters would once again be expected to use their license in the public interest. What is needed is the busting of media trusts. There is danger of censorship. But there is also the reality of monopoly, exercised by large corporate interests which keep the public from knowing what is going on in their own society. What is needed is media education so that people will not be helpless illiterates in their media world. What is needed is public action against sponsors, agencies, networks, and stations which will form the countervailing economic force that pits the public's interest against industry's profit motive. What is needed are new ideas and approaches in how to use these media in ways that can open up their potential for the public commonweal.

The Carnegie Commission on the Future of Public Broadcasting in 1979 challenged the country to rethink its vision of what broadcasting could be:

> The United States is the only Western nation relying so exclusively upon advertising effectiveness as the gatekeeper of its broadcasting activities. The consequences of using the public spectrum primarily for commercial purposes are numerous, and increasingly disturbing. The idea of broadcasting as a force in the public interest, a display case for the best of America's creative arts, a forum of public debate—advancing the democratic conversation and enhancing the public imagination—has receded before the inexorable force of audience maximization.[11]

In all probability it will be necessary for us to go to the economic roots of the problem before solutions become workable. Government will need to perform new roles in subsidizing alternatives to the communication media we now have. It will have to provide a substantial and continuing financial base for public broadcasting. It will be required to create and maintain an open marketplace of ideas.

Open communication is necessary to our social structure, and essential to maintaining national stability as well as allowing for social reform. We cannot hope to approach the problems of the 21st century in America successfully until our communication processes are genuinely open and the original meaning and intent of the First Amendment two centuries ago is realized in the communication media of today.

ELEVEN

U.S. MEDIA:
THE WHOLE WORLD
IS WATCHING

Freedom of the press is reserved for those who own one.

A. J. Liebling

Between the weak and the strong, it is freedom which oppresses and the law which frees.

Jean Batiste Lacourdaire (1872)

Not long ago a friend of mine arrived in New York City to take a job with the American Bible Society. He had come from Vancouver. Although he was a very media-wise person, the communication scene amazed him. "Half the people in New York City are doing nothing all day but producing, moving, or working with information," he said. "It's incredible!"

He was speaking the literal truth. Today more than half of the total labor force in the United States is involved in the production, dissemination, or use of information in its various forms. Almost half of the U.S. gross national product is generated by information-related activities.

The same thing is happening worldwide. The amount of raw information in the world now doubles in less than a decade. *The Wall Street Journal* today uses satellite to transmit its pages to seven regional printing plants throughout the United States, and it prints its Hong Kong edition the same way. The *International Herald Tribune* daily transfers its pages via satellite from Paris to its printing plant in Hong Kong and at the same time prints identical pages in London and Zurich.

Media and the New Colonialism

The significance of this shift from a commodity-based to an information-based society is far more than that it allows us to buy the same newspaper almost anywhere in the world. It means that we already have moved into an age where information is power—economic, political, and social power.

Of course, information always has been power. Two thousand years ago the Roman roads throughout southern Europe gave the emperors the information and transportation they required to hold the empire together. A thousand years ago knots tied in strings carried by runners along the Andes Mountains enabled the Incas to run their domain. A hundred years ago the lines of international communication closely followed the lines of the North Atlantic empires. The cartel of European news agencies divided up the world according to the political and economic spheres of influence. Just as roads communication held the Roman and Incan Empires together, so transoceanic cables and later radio frequencies provided the links of empires 50 years ago.

Even when the post–World War II national liberation movements changed the political alignment of the world, the old structures of economic and information dependence persisted. And as the Third World nations threw off political domination, the First World nations simply substituted economic and media domination. In fact, as the production, control, and use of information has become increasingly important during the last few years, information dependency in the Third World has actually increased.

Where and how does this dependency take place?

First, there is dependency in the press. Two U.S. news agencies dominate the entire world's daily output. The Associated Press puts out *17 million* words overseas daily, serving 108 nations with 559 foreign correspondents and 62 foreign bureaus. United Press International operates in 92 countries including 2,246 subscribers outside the United States, plus 36 national news agencies. It produces 11 million words and 200 news pictures daily and gathers its foreign news with a staff of 578 overseas and 81 foreign bureaus.

The other press agencies—AFP (France), Reuters (United Kingdom), Tass (Soviet Union) and a half-dozen other national press groups—taken together, issue some 3 million words daily—about one-tenth of the output of the two U.S. agencies.

Second, there is dependency in radio and television. All broadcasting is controlled to some extent by governments, partly because the frequencies are limited and must be regulated to avoid chaos, but more importantly because radio and television are such powerful agents for shaping culture.

Again, U.S. broadcasting dominates the world scene. UNESCO estimates that the number of hours of American TV programs exported each year ranges up to 200,000, or more than twice the number of hours exported by all the other nations combined. Anyone who has seen "Kojak" and "The Bionic Woman" in Hong Kong, or "Peyton Place" and "The Flintstones" in Latin America knows what this means.

Third, there is dependency because of advertising. By 1970, only 2 of the top 25 U.S. advertising agencies did *not* have overseas offices. In Peru, for example, more than 80% of the advertising carried by Peruvian newspapers, radio, and television is channeled through big American advertising firms, such as J. Walter Thompson, McKann Erickson, Grant Advertising, and Katts Acciones, Inc.

One of the most serious problems created by First World domination of advertising in the Third World is that it tends to create a consumer demand for luxury products. Disposable diapers, cosmetics, and soft drinks are pressed on the population in nations which desperately need to promote the basics of good health and consumption of simple, nutritious foods.

For example, in the early 1980s Nestle ads widely circulated in Africa showed a "nurse" urging young mothers to buy and use powdered-milk formula (a major Nestle product) for their children. As a result of this advertising campaign many mothers shifted from breast-feeding to bottle feeding. When mothers discovered they could no longer breast-feed their children they had to rely totally on the Nestle product. But since most of the families were desperately poor, mothers began to water down the milk. As a result, some babies died because of unsterile water, bottles, and nipples, and many others simply died of starvation, while parents looked on helplessly. Churches in Europe and North America negotiated with Nestle to get them to withdraw the ad campaign. Nestle refused. The courts proved to be useless because

Nestle had operations in many different countries, outside the jurisdiction of any single national legal system. So the churches launched a boycott of Nestle products which, over a three-year period, resulted in Nestle finally withdrawing the ads. This is but one example of the way media domination results in advertising which benefits the industrialized Western nations at the expense of the poor.

Fourth, media domination occurs in data flow. This is the least understood, yet potentially the most important aspect of information dependency. During the past 30 years the world's basic industries—textiles, steel, automobiles, and rubber—have slowly been replaced by the new industries—electronics, space, biochemistry, and exploitation of the seas. All the new industries depend heavily on the processing of information. Cees Hamelink of the Institute of Social Studies in the Netherlands estimates that the costs of industrial production today are approximately 70% for the processing of information (market exploitation, advertising, research and development, and especially for intracompany communications.)

The new companies are not "located" anywhere. They place their various production, distribution, marketing, and finance centers anywhere in the world which best suits them. The corporation was an economic and legal concept invented in the 19th century to avoid the problem of personal accountability. Its creation facilitated the accumulation of capital which resulted in the economic system we know today. The successor to the corporation is the multinational corporation, which was developed after World War II and soon emerged as an ingenious way for individuals to avoid the problem of *any* accountability, since it stood outside the jurisdiction of any single nation.

Multinationals transcend national boundaries and therefore are mostly outside national control. They exist beyond the laws and regulations of state and federal governments, which until the 1970s were used by societies to control the excessive power of huge business enterprises. Their computers, data banks, terminals, programs, and software provide them with the power to move money, labor, parts, and natural resources in ways to emphasize profits without consideration of the welfare of any nation, especially the new Third World nations and their peoples.

Finally, there is media dependency in satellite transmission and sensing. Satellites are the electronic highways which make the other information technologies possible. Worldwide news services, television programs, and data flow would be impossible without the satellite. And whoever controls the satellites controls the world's information flow.

For example, Chase Manhattan Bank in New York can keep watch on crops and shipping, the mining of resources, weather developments, and many other aspects of business in most of the nations of the world— daily, hourly—right from their offices in Manhattan. If the Landsat Satellite picks up a different color in its pictures of the coffee plantations of Colombia, Chase Manhattan's specialists may determine that this indicates a blight on the leaves which will result in serious crop failure. This information then allows Chase's investment department to buy and sell coffee futures *that day* on the world's markets with information that even the coffee growers in the plantations in Colombia may not yet have! This is what it means to say that knowledge is power.

In theory, anyone can purchase those pictures from the Landsat Satellite, though they are costly. But to have the computer lines and terminals, specialists in image analysis, specialists in food production, geology, land management, ocean ecology, investment specialists, and, finally, to own the worldwide satellite facilities to move the information instantly—such capability can be achieved only by very large, multinational corporations.

The result is that the technological era in communications is benefiting the rich at the expense of the poor, which raises some important moral questions. By what right do some get to benefit from the new technology at the expense of others? If taxes pay for the research and development that makes the new communication technology available, should not the taxpayers have a say in how the technology is to be used? And if the technology depends on the use of scarce spectrum which belongs to everyone equally, should not everyone benefit equally from its use?

A New World-Information Order

As nation after nation in Asia and Africa gained independence in the 1950s, it became apparent to these newly "free" nations that the old political colonialism had largely been replaced by new economic and information colonialism. In 1956 the leaders of most of the former colonies of the world met in Bandung to organize a "nonaligned" movement which established their group as a buffer between the proponents of capitalism (First World) and those of communism (Second World). This Third World group, interested in neither capitalism or communism so much as in the opportunity to develop their own nationhood, began to press for a new economic independence from both First and Second Worlds. The United Nations was their forum.

By 1970, the 16th General Assembly of UNESCO had defined the concept of a New International Economic Order which stated that the emerging nations would not be able to develop until they decreased their economic dependence on the First World. By this time the members of UNESCO were aware that the economic well-being of the Third World also depended upon a new kind of information flow. The Universal Declaration of Human Rights, adopted in San Francisco at the time of the founding of the United Nations, stated the goal in Article 19:

> Everyone has the right to freedom of opinion and expression; this right includes freedom to hold opinions without interference and to seek, receive and impart information and ideas through any media regardless of frontiers.[1]

In 1974 the nonaligned nations had started their own News Pool, an attempt to redress the imbalance of news about the Third World. Charging U.S. news agencies with intentional bias and systematic distortion, Rafael Caldera, former President of Venezuela, said: "Perhaps the phrase 'no news is good news' has become 'good news is no news.' Only the most deplorable incidents, be they the work of nature or man, get reported." Venezuelan President Carlos Andres Perez agreed: "The big press of the big countries does not report about our realities, our struggles and our goals. . . ."

In 1976 a UNESCO conference outlined the basic proposals of a New International Information Order: greater public access and participation in the media, regional cooperation in news flow, and agreement on a *"free and balanced flow"* of information.

It was this last concept which became the center of debate in the West. At present, the nations of the world are divided on how information should be treated. There are basically two views. One view, supported primarily by the United States, Great Britain, and most of the European nations, calls for a "free flow" of information, that is, virtually no governmental restrictions except technical ones; in effect communication flow exists for those who are willing and able to pay for it, and who claim it first.

The second view, supported primarily by the new Third World nations, questions this de facto dominance of communication by the West, and calls for a "balanced flow," which means that laws would require a balance of First World and Third World perspectives. An example is Tunisia's Ambassador Mustapha Masmoudi's call in 1980 for the establishment of national communication agencies which would be responsible for "formulating overall communications policies" to promote national development. He urged information professionals to draw up a "code of ethics governing the conduct of all communicators," including the requirement "that the events be reported in their real context," and to provide for recourse and "the right of response to and correction of misstatements."

But when in 1980 UNESCO agencies began to talk "balance," Western news agencies, and especially U.S. news agencies, began to cry foul. *Time* magazine carried an essay entitled "The Global First Amendment War," saying that "at stake, ultimately, is the right of readers, radio listeners and television viewers everywhere to be properly [sic] informed about the world around them; for the developing and industrial countries alike to learn about one another without hindrance."[2] To this Urho Kekkonen, President of Finland, replied: "Freedom of speech has also become in practice the freedom of the rich."

To complicate matters further, the communist bloc has supported the "balanced flow" position in UNESCO. But media "balance" within these nations usually means whatever the government decrees, and there is almost no opportunity for the presentation of other views to help provide balance. Thus the Second World support for "balance" is probably more of a political ploy to appear to be aligned with the Third World nations than it is genuine support for the concept.

The issue of "free flow" versus "balanced flow" is perplexing, particularly for Americans with our concept of First Amendment guarantee of free speech as central to our idea of governance. Many would say that there is no principle more central to our liberty than the freedom of citizens to communicate with one another, and that this freedom must never be encroached upon by government for any reason, no matter how benign.

On the other hand, as Third World leaders point out, the 18th and 19th century laissez-faire concept in economics, which encouraged Europe and America to act in any way that favored their own self-interest, clearly resulted in massive injustices throughout the world. This same big-fish-eat-little-fish morality has also been at work in the field of communication. Can laws and international agreements help to restrain unfair media competition?

The current debate on this question is full of ironies. Many of the Third World nations most vocal in calling for "balanced" information are themselves dictatorships or oligopolies which use information to further the interests of a tiny power elite. Korea, much of the Soviet bloc, and many nations in South America and Africa use the press mostly as a propaganda tool. On the other hand, the United States, the loudest voice calling for "free flow," maintains such a thorough domination of many foreign markets that a genuine free flow of information is impossible there as well.

In 1978 UNESCO established an International Commission for the Study of Communication Problems. This 16-member body, with representation from First, Second, and Third World nations and led by former Irish Foreign Minister Sean MacBride, made its report in November 1980. The MacBride Report challenges the thesis held by many in the West that technology is neutral, and notes that usually technology is part of a system which favors the most power groups in *any* given society. It suggested that some technology ought to be delayed or even indefinitely postponed if it clearly fails to further the needs of humankind.[3]

Unfortunately, the MacBride Report as a whole failed to provide any definitive proposals to meet the demands of either side. On one hand, editors of the *New York Times* were upset because the report seemed to suggest some kind of government intervention to achieve balance. On the other hand, Third World nations regretted that the report provided no clear call for laws or international agreements to end the present economic domination by First World nations.

The Issues: Freedom, Justice, and Profits

What are the issues involved that cause such strong reaction from the communication industry as well as First- and Third World nations? They are freedom, justice, and money—as viewed from the different perspectives of the First and Third Worlds.

Freedom

Our First Amendment guarantees of a free press and free speech are among the most cherished rights in America, and for good reason. One has only to live a few months in a country whose press is dominated by government edict to recognize how stultifying and repressive it can be. The Western tradition of press freedom is indispensable to individual well-being and to the democratic process.

In recent years, however, there has arisen a kind of mystical attraction to the principle of free speech, an awe and obeisance which society normally reserves for its objects of worship. It is as though "free speech" were a kind of first principle—self-evident, self-validating, deserving of unquestioned loyalty. But surely it is dangerous to deify any ethical principle, even one so important as the idea that speech ought to be unequivocally free.

There are three reasons why it is dangerous to absolutize free speech. One is that free speech is not an ultimate good, but rather an instrumental good. James Madison, that staunch advocate of free speech, insisted that the right of people to speak and to listen is not an end in itself, but is a means of achieving "popular government," by which he meant the democratic process whereby people have the opportunity to take a real part in the decisions which affect their lives. In some cases, an *absolute* right to speak could actually subvert and defeat that democratic process, such as the "right" of an advertiser to misinform the public, or the "right" of a broadcaster to attack someone without allowing an opportunity for that person to reply. Laws and regulations have been enacted that make these "rights" illegal—and they were enacted to further the intent of the First Amendment, not to defeat it. When tested, these laws and regulations have been declared constitutional by the highest court in the land. Free speech is important, but not absolute, because it is merely instrumental to the higher good of democracy.

Second, the right of free speech should not be absolutized because it then becomes self-contradictory. Constitutional lawyer Ronald Dworkin points out that "every extension of the First Amendment is, from the standpoint of democracy, a double-edged sword. It enhances democracy because public information increases the general power of the public. *But it also contracts democracy because any constitutional right*

disables the popularly elected legislature from enacting some legis-
lation it might otherwise wish to enact, and this decreases the general
power of the public."[4]

Dworkin argues that the support of free speech as a requirement for democracy demands, by its own logic, "some threshold line to be drawn between interpretations of the First Amendment that would protect and those that would invade democracy." This, he believes, is what the Supreme Court does when it describes, in general terms, "what manner of invasion of the powers of the press would so constrict the flow of information to the public as to leave the public unable intelligently to decide whether to overturn [any particular] limitation of the press by further legislation." To absolutize the right of free speech would prevent the Supreme Court from *ever* drawing the line between invasion of necessary rights and the protection of democracy, and thus would make it self-contradictory.

Third, free speech ought not be absolutized because the First Amendment basically protects not the right of the press to speak, but the *right of every citizen to know.* The courts have made this distinction clear. For example, Byron White, in his opinion on behalf of a unanimous decision of the Supreme Court in the landmark Red Lion case, said that "it is the right of the viewers and listeners, not the right of the broadcasters, which is paramount."[5] That is, the broadcaster has only a derivative right to communicate, derived from the right of the citizen to *know.*

This is one of the best-kept secrets in American broadcasting: if, in exercising his or her rights, the broadcaster violates the First Amendment rights of the viewers or listeners—their right to know, to receive information, to have access to a diversity of viewpoints—then the viewer's or listener's rights come *first.*

Of course, the newspaper trusts are not subject to the restrictions that apply to broadcasters. However, from these points it can be argued that if a "free" press were to become so economically or politically powerful that it could actually *withhold* or *distort* news and information to such an extent that citizens no longer could participate as equals in the process of governing themselves, then citizens should expect our government, through the courts or the legislature, to take steps to create new sources of news and information and to curb the monopoly power of that so-called "free" press.

Howard C. Anawalt, a professor of constitutional law at the University of Santa Clara, studied the MacBride Report and concluded that the proposals of the commission were consistent with the U.S. Constitution:

> The Commission approach offers both a physical foundation and a set of protective principles for development of a worldwide communication freedom. It passes the basic test of compatibility with United States constitutional norms. Informed United States criticism should therefore take the tack of seeking to improve the proposed new order, rather than rejecting it altogether.[6]

Justice

A second issue has to do with justice—in this case, justice for the emerging new nations of the Third World. How is it possible to get genuine communication flowing where there is very little of it to start with? This is the dilemma facing the Third World countries, many of which have no indigenous press at all, but only a remnant of colonial news sources—perhaps a small news-and-information outlet in the capital city for the urban elite, plus incoming shortwave broadcasts from the superpowers, available to those with batteries and radios.

Frank Campbell, information minister of Guyana, has responded to Western charges that the new information order would give UNESCO jurisdiction over the news media:

> The issue is not UNESCO controlling the media. The question is [how] to have a basis of communication other than a purely commercial one and communication ethics based on something other than ethnocentricity and historical arrogance. We are not saying UNESCO should issue a license saying you must have so many stories coming out of Guyana, Tanzania or India, and what these stories must say.[7]

First Amendment advocates in America must face the fact that imposition of our highly industrialized model of big press as a check on the excesses of big government has very limited relevance to many places in the Third World where there is little literacy and practically no economic market for news which could help create a large mass press. Furthermore, our insistence on absolute freedom or a "free flow" of information is seen by the developing nations as the freedom of the fox in the chicken coop.

Campbell speaks eloquently for the Third World:

> By a free press, in the West, you mean a press owned by a few people who have a commercial monopoly, really a monopoly of the conscience of mankind. They are "the good people" and they "know what is right." A free press means, for you, that the owner of the press is free to prevent whom he wants from being heard. You don't have a free press at all. You have a press imprisoned by commercial interests.[8]

It is difficult for people in the United States to understand that government *can* have a legitimate role in communication. In Western Europe, however, almost every nation has a long tradition of government-related broadcast organizations and information agencies, most of which are highly respected. The BBC was established by Parliament and depends on its levy of a set tax. Its news service is widely respected throughout the world. Sveriges Radio in Sweden has a similar governmental tie. Broadcasting in Germany is the creature of the individual *Lander* (states). Japan has a mix of commercial and noncommercial broadcasting, and Japan's NHK, one of the most-respected news organizations in the world, was created and is sustained by government edict.

Of course, governmental dominance of news and information too often has been the handmaiden of dictatorship, oligopoly, and general repression. There is a great deal of hypocrisy among many leaders of the Third World and the U.S.S.R. in calling for a free and balanced flow of information when there is a nonexistent flow of news and information between the power elite and the masses in their own nations. Certainly UNESCO must be as critical of political constraints as it is of economic and cultural constraints on news flow, and the MacBride Report makes these dangers abundantly clear. But to insist on rigidly applying our own historically derived concepts of press freedom to the Third World, and to reject out of hand any possible role of government insuring the free flow of news and information, is in fact unfaithful to the principle of democracy which underlies our own First Amendment.

Profits

The third major issue in the debate is profits. The commercialization of news and information is being seriously questioned, both domestically and overseas.

Many Third World leaders have a strong bias against free enterprise as the system to rely upon for maintenance of the communication process that undergirds their national destiny. This anticommercialism causes the U.S. media to see red: they are certain that behind the bias lurks the long arm of Soviet control or, at the very least, that it represents a tilt toward communism.

It is true that for many years the U.S.S.R. has used the communication issue to turn the Third World against the First. But this is only a small part of the story. The nonaligned nations themselves have seen what commercialism in the media has done to the flow of news and information overseas, what it has done in the United States, and what—to some extent—it already is doing within their own countries.

They see that in the United States the broadcast and print media have increasingly turned viewers and readers into a product to be delivered to the sponsors, so that the objective of news has changed from informing, enlightening, and entertaining simply to reaching and holding the largest audience regardless of the damage done to other journalistic objectives.

All of this comes naturally to a system which deals with news and information as a means to a commercial end, and the American public has become so accustomed to this narrow point of view that we simply do not see the distortions and the filtering out of "non-American" messages. But such systematic distortion, immediately recognized by the Third World nations, is a valid reason why they have pressed so hard for a document stating a preference for "noncommercial forms of mass communication," as they have done in UNESCO. Although the UNESCO statements make no mention of anticommercialism, the MacBride Report proposes in Recommendation 58 that "effective legal measures should be designed to: limit the process of concentration and monopolization; [and] . . . reduce the influence of advertising upon editorial policy and broadcast programming."[9]

The strong reaction of the U.S. delegation to such proposals makes it clear what the real priorities of our government are with regard to scope, balance, depth, and fairness in news and information, on the one hand, and profits for business, on the other. When the State Department considers whom it will appoint to international conferences that deal with such matters, it consistently turns to the representatives of the communication industry rather than to knowledgeable representatives from public-interest groups. Thus the government really has *no* policy in the sense of a position arrived at through elected representatives or referendums. Instead, the public is "represented" by the largest businesses which stand to make the most profit from those arrangements that benefit their special interests.

Some Guiding Ethical Principles

In dealing with a subject so complex and being played for such large stakes, what guiding principles might we consider in moving toward a more just and equitable worldwide communication system?

1. *The basic objective of public communication should be to enable people to participate fully in their own development and the development of their nation.* A structure or process which hinders that objective—whether it is political, economic, ideological, or social—should be rejected. Control by special interest—whether in the name of capitalism or communism, supporting a monopoly or a dictatorship, reflecting the views of a single individual or a group—must be weeded out in the interests of maximum diversity of expression.

2. *Government has a role in maintaining the rights of citizenship.* The question of private versus state ownership and control must be secondary to the creation and maintenance of communication systems that facilitate genuine democratization. Every individual in every nation has the right to know. This means that every just society has the responsibility to create those conditions in which each citizen is able to take part in politics intelligently and as the equal of any other. People must have the technical means both to speak and to listen if they are to participate in the process of governing themselves, and a major role of government lies in securing and protecting these means.

3. *Third World nations should be allowed to develop their own self-reliance in news, information, and entertainment, progressing at a rate and in a manner appropriate to their needs rather than in conformity to the marketplace needs of the industrialized nations.* We ought consciously to reject the temptation to take communication models of the developed nations and try to make them "fit" the Third World. Rather, whole new forms of communication, appropriate for developing nations, need to be devised. We must ask: What are the existing communication processes in the nation, and how can they be improved and developed?

One of the misunderstandings which naturally arise among people of goodwill in the First World is that the problems of the Third World can be solved "if only we can get enough of the new technology." This is the fallacy of the "technological fix." In reality, advanced information technology is *not* the real solution to the current social problems of the Third World nations. Indeed, technical innovation must never be equated automatically with social progress. The poverty and health problems in the Third World are not going to be solved by computers but by a different set of political, economic, and social structures. Alvin Toffler's exuberant Third Wave prediction of a nirvana wrought by the new communications technology completely misunderstands the situation. He ignores the fact that technology represents power, and that the existing power relationships will tend to be extended and further entrenched by multinationals and governments which control the technology. The real danger, as Amory Lovins suggests, is that it will be all too easy to spread darkness at the speed of light. The real solutions are far more fundamental, and these are the solutions that the debate in UNESCO is all about, and is why the large information structures in the United States and the West generally are so upset about them. Unless the power structures themselves are changed, the technological innovations will only make the situation worse.

Simple, inexpensive media such as radio, local telephones, and newspapers may suit the needs of a developing nation far better than television, satellites, and big-city newspapers. Our objective should be maximum participation and maximum sources and diversity of information, not maximun̉ profits for large communication conglomerates or maximum political control for a tiny power elite.

In considering its strategy for what would best suit the communication needs of the Third World (and much of the First and Second Worlds as well), the World Association for Christian Communication (WACC) has concluded that "group media" must have a high priority. WACC is channeling less of its funds into large shortwave services and large publishing houses, and more into the development of small printing presses, the production of audiocassettes, local drama and music groups, and the use of communication forms indigenous to the village life, such as storytelling, puppets, and mime.

It is revealing that the audiocassette and videocassette, small mimeographed newspapers and local radio played a significant role in the popular uprising against Ferdinand Marcos in the Philippines. In the

Union of South Africa, where the government has limited the access in the black townships to FM radio which covers a small area and can be controlled by the government, the development of small local newspapers has been one of the few ways the black citizens can "talk" to one another. Studies have demonstrated that for many poor regions of the world, the introduction of a simple telephone into the village can result in major increases in income. Telephone connection to the outside world allows villagers to plan where to send their crops for maximum profit, to learn what are the going prices, and to arrange for transportation—simple advantages which may spell the difference between profit and loss for the whole village.

In sum, just as there must come a new world-economic order, *there must come a new world-communication order.* Its goal will be to enable people everywhere to guide their own future. It will take time, but it will come. We are living in a world in which we become each moment increasingly interdependent, and in which exploitation of others becomes increasingly self-destructive. Today there is no place we can run from the consequences of our actions.

If this new communication order *is* truly coming, then we in the United States must be in the forefront, making it happen. And even if it is *not* imminent, we must work toward making the goal a reality in the name of our own religious and political commitment to freedom and justice for all.

TWELVE

SIGNS OF HOPE

Christians are not those who are being saved out of
the world but those who know that the world is being
saved.

H. Richard Niebuhr

We have come a long way in our understanding of television during
the last 30 years. In 1960, Joseph T. Klapper, then the acknowledged
leader in television research, solemnly declared "it has been pretty
well demonstrated that the mass media do not serve as the primary
determinant or even as a very important determinant of any of the basic
attitudes or the basic behavior patterns of either children or adults.[1]
Now we know that the advertisers were right when they bet that television does have a powerful influence on the attitudes and behavior of
almost everyone, and that the cumulative effect of television as the
cultivator of society is yet to be completely assessed.

We know that consumers are strongly attached to "free TV," but
also that they spend an enormous sum supporting it, through the purchase of their TV sets, the cost of electricity, and the add-on costs to
every item they purchase which is advertised, not to mention the lost
revenue in tax-deductible billions spent by advertisers.

We know that television entertains us, a companion ever ready with
the escape and fantasy we occasionally need, but also that it cultivates
a mean world full of violence, that its values and stories demean and
dehumanize us, and that its religious impact is the very antithesis of
the Christian faith in which most people in our society profess to
believe.

We know that television informs us, a genuine window on the world,
but also that its commercial demand for profit severely limits the
amount of diversity of opinion that is aired, that it tends to trivialize
issues and to represent the views of the rich, with the result that through

192

TV the average citizen simply cannot get the information needed to make intelligent decisions about living in our democracy.

We know that television moves our goods and is the backbone of our mass production and marketing system, but also that the system works at the expense of truth and justice both here and around the world, that it is being used to expand and maintain cultural and economic domination over much of the Third World, and is enormously wasteful of both natural and human resources.

At the same time, we have come to recognize that the traditional forms of church communication today play a very minor and peripheral role in the total communication mix of the society. The Sunday sermon is a one-way form of communication which confronts a highly self-selective audience with a style no longer in use anywhere else in the culture. The church school depends upon nonprofessional volunteers, is presumptuous in its schedule and miniscule in its effect, while at the same time prodigiously wasteful of expensive classroom space which often lies unused 99% of the time. The actions of national church bodies belie seriousness, pretending action while only issuing pronouncements which are systematically ignored by the churches, the press, and society.

What Can We Do?

The solution that is put forward by some religious leaders is that the church should become much more actively involved in the media of our time. They cite the change which occurred in communication technology during the 15th century, when the invention of printing vastly increased the distribution of the Scriptures, and acted as a catalyst for major reformation in the church. Now, they say, we have had another media revolution—television has taken over as the primary communication locus in society—and once again the church must come aboard and reinterpret the tradition of the Christian religion, this time in television, the medium of the age.

The printing press indeed changed the culture's perception of how to deal with religious experience. Religion became much more amenable to linear analysis, to objectification as something on a printed page, to doctrines and heresies and bureaucratization. And it is true that the communications revolution we are passing through is fully as radical as that of the 15th century.

But television is likely to do for religious experience today something quite different from what the invention of printing did for it five hundred years ago. There is an intrinsic connection between the medium and the message, between the "how" and the "what" of religious communication. The cultural effect of inexpensive duplication of words on a page is wholly different from the cultural effect of inexpensive transmission of the *moving image* by electricity.

William Kuhns has put today's problem very clearly: "The entertainment milieu has transformed the ways in which we believe and are capable of believing. An absolute kind of belief, as well as a belief in absolutes, becomes increasingly difficult as the entertainment milieu trains people to believe tentatively and with elasticity.[2] Kuhns understands that "the very concept of faith—to believe in that which you cannot see and cannot understand—comes with difficulty to a generation which has depended, as perhaps no generation before, on its senses."[3] Avery Dulles presses this point further by asking whether, if faith depends on hearing, as it did for those of the first-century church, faith is still possible for those whose psyche has been predominantly formed by the image industries.[4]

Also, in this book I have held that television is not simply a technology but an entire *system* involving an economic philosophy, a political structure, and strong cultural interconnections. There is no way we can separate the media's technological possibilities from its economic-political-cultural realities. I have shown how this system called television is remarkably fashioned to resist change by effectively distributing responsibility so that, in the end, no one is in charge, no one is responsible, there is no central point from which changes can be made. At the same time, I have maintained that *everyone* shares some of the responsibility for what we make of television—since it exists through our support and it resonates our values—and that therefore effective change will require a modification of the entire cultural system of which we are a part.

For these reasons, television cannot be considered simply a "resource" which Christians, in an exercise of good stewardship, can use to "advance the kingdom." Television is an amalgam of technology, power, and values which is far too resistant to being "used" by any ideology other than the ideology which formed it and which it is designed to maintain: the technological era. The system we call television *is* the utilitarian value system of "what works is good"—a system that values the ends of effectiveness and efficiency at the expense of human ends.

To engage with such a powerful system in ways other than what I have called creative transformation strategies, and through media reform, is doomed to be capitulation, not communication. In fact, the attempt to *use* television uncritically is a prime example of what Frederick Ferre has called our "technolatry," the belief that "every apparent evil brought on by technique is to be countered by yet greater faith in technique."

Television already has succeeded in transforming most cultural institutions and activities to meet its own needs and to fit its own imagery. Sports, education, entertainment, politics—all have become subservient to the demands of television, rather than the other way around. If religion attempts uncritically to "use" television and thus partake of its vast power, it too will become co-opted and transformed to meet the needs and imagery of television.

The electronic church is the obvious example of where this cooptation already has taken place. Unfortunately, a number of mainline denominations persist in trying to mimic these electronic evangelists, in their objectives if not their precise techniques. They continue to experiment with high-budget TV specials, with the purchase of television stations or satellite transponders, with the development of cable networks—all aimed at reaching mass audiences with "the gospel message." But they expect too much from the mass media and not enough from the church. Communication leaders in the mainline churches would be much more faithful to the demands of the gospel if they were to accept the limitations of the mass media, and then help other church leaders devise a total communication strategy for the churches in which mass media took its rightful place alongside worship services, group processes, retreats, occasions for fellowship, service, education and mission—in other words, as a part of the whole life and witness of the church.

Understanding communication—its process, its power, and in particular its manifestations in the mass media—demands changes in the church. It requires it to consider wholly new types of ministries, new languages and images, rethinking the place of the pulpit, inventing new forms of worship, the redefinition of jobs and the reassignment of personnel. To treat communication in the church as if it were public relations is both faulty theology and inept administration.

Seminaries, especially, need to devote much more attention to the task of working out what it means to proclaim the *skandalon* of the gospel to a generation which has no background knowledge of the gospel, how to create community in a society where the old forms of community have become fragmented and dysfunctional, and how to communicate within a culture where the mass media have devalued genuine communication in the name of communication.

The church has depended for too long on ineffective modes of communication. In its accommodation to the print medium it has become dependent upon logical, analytical, deductive, and abstract modes of thinking. It has tended to confuse words with action, verbal solutions with real solutions, and sermons preached with sermons heard. If Christianity is essentially a faith to be shared, and if the Christian churches take seriously the possibilities of using what we know about the process of communication, then its task is to establish environments which allow people to communicate with each other, with their own leaders, and with the world. These environments do not exclude the mass media, but neither do they depend upon them. The essence of these environments is that they be interpersonal, interactive, and involving. In the words of Avery Dulles, "the most effective way for the Church to teach, in our day, is more by being and doing than by defining and commanding."[5]

But television is neither interpersonal, interactive, nor involving. Therefore, what I am proposing is not that society do away with television, but rather that people be enabled to take it or leave it. People must be able to understand the power of television sufficiently so they can *use it* when they desire escape, relaxation, information, entertainment—which are perfectly legitimate human needs—but not be *used by it.*

This is the chief value of developing a critical attitude toward television viewing: in the process of viewing, discussing, evaluating, and just plain leaving it alone, we become something which television itself does not encourage. We become *active participants rather than passive receivers.* We begin to raise questions about the "given" world of television. Through a change in our attitude toward television, we can turn a closed, one-way system into a two-way process through group discussion and action and through response to stations and producers. And if we apply our worldview, or, for Christians, our theological and biblical criteria, in a reasonably rigorous way, we can free ourselves from the tyranny of the television tube.

What Kind of Society Do We Want?

As we consider how to deal with the world of television, the basic question is, What kind of society do we really want? Robert Bellah has argued that this question remains largely unanswered in America today, because for two centuries we have kept in tension two quite different views of society. One view is that we are a republic, a nation characterized by public participation in the exercise of power, political equality of its citizens, a wide distribution of property with few very rich or very poor, customs of public-spirited involvement, and a willingness of citizens to sacrifice their own interests for the common good.

The other view is that we are a liberal constitutional regime in which the good society results from the action of citizens following their own self-interests, organized through the proper mechanisms that balance these conflicting interests, with the state operating only as caretaker, a referee maintaining public order and allowing the economic market-mechanisms and the free market in ideas to produce wealth and happiness. The first emphasizes the public, communal life; the second the private, individualistic life. Both views are embedded in our national history—the republican view more in the Declaration of Independence, where Jefferson in its opening lines refers to "the laws of nature and of nature's God" that stand above and judge the laws of men; and the liberal view more in the Constitution, where there is no reference to God at all, and the emphasis is upon the balancing of powers.[6]

Since liberalism is dominant in the Constitution, where did the nation get its sense of value and purpose? It got it from religion, first during the Great Awakening of the 1740s, when religious revivalism inspired the sense of national community which made possible the formation of a new nation, and later in what Bellah calls "public theology," with its theme that Americans are the "chosen people." This public theology, contained in most speeches of the founders, had no legal status, but without it the national community could not have survived. Said John Adams during his first year as vice president: "Our constitution was made only for a moral and a religious people. It is wholly inadequate to the government of any other."[7] Madison stated in 1785,

"Before any man can be considered as a member of Civil Society, he must be considered as a subject of the Governor of the Universe. . . ." And George Washington affirmed in his farewell address: "Of all the suppositions and habits which lead to political prosperity Religion and morality are indispensable supports. . . . The mere Politician, equally with the pious man ought to respect and cherish them."[8]

In the 1830s Alexis de Tocqueville observed that the school for republican virtue in America was not the schools and universities, but the churches. More than the laws or the physical circumstances of the country, said Tocqueville, it was the mores that contributed to the success of the American democracy, and the mores were rooted in religion. Tocqueville saw that naked self-interest was certain to destroy the republic, and that religion could be the great restraining element to turn self-interest into public-spirited sacrifice for the general welfare.[9]

During the last two decades Bellah has analyzed the current national values and mores and finds them moving away from the republican ideal of the public welfare and toward the liberal ideal of individual self-interest. As a sociologist, he sees "the balance of American religious life slipping away from those denominations that have a historic concern for the common good toward religious groups so privatistic and self-centered that they begin to approach the consumer cafeteria model. . . ."[10] He asks whether it is possible for America to survive as a republic, or whether the republican ideal has been eroded beyond repair. And, if this latter is the case, then he believes that one or another kind of authoritarian regime is likely to replace the traditions both of republicanism and of liberal constitutionalism.

This analysis of the nature of our national foundations is important, because just as it was the function of religion in the early days of the republic to provide the moral vision which gave the nation its cohesion and impetus, so *now that role is increasingly being assumed by television*. The difference is ominous. One is rooted in the lives of individuals in the context of the worshiping community; the other is rooted in an economic system interested only in profits, with a technology interested only in results. The one is committed to community and the ideal of self-sacrifice for the greater good of the commonweal; the other is committed to utilitarianism and to the development of technology for the purpose of instantly gratifying the needs of the individual.

In the biblical tradition, the key word for understanding individual motivation is "conscience." In the utilitarian tradition the key word is "self-interest." It is both significant and distressing that the most visible attempt to harmonize these two conflicting traditions today is the electronic church, which corrupts the biblical tradition by offering a Bible-based rhetoric that obscures its real message of utilitarian individualism. This private pietism, emphasizing individual rewards and at the expense of social responsibility, extends from Norman Vincent Peale in the mid-20th century, to Reverend Ike, Jim Bakker, and Robert Schuller today. It is acutely painful to biblical religion today, because many people, seeking a way to express their conscience in society, are led to reject any "religious" expression of it because they identify these corruptions of the biblical tradition with *all* religious expression.

We cannot have it both ways. Until now our country has managed to hold both liberal constitutionalism and the republican ideal in an uneasy balance, in part because the contribution of religion has been so strong. But today organized religion is losing its cultural influence to the multiple threats posed by the technological era and especially to its embodiment in commercial television. With television commanding more of people's time than any activity other than work and sleep, and with an instantly accessible, enormously appealing alternate worldview, religion and its worldview is losing the battle for the soul of the nation.

What is required is much more serious attention to the role of television, and at the same time a revitalization of the role of religion in American life. The only way we are going to deal effectively with television is by refusing to accept it as a given, and to place it into proper perspective. But unless we have a way of standing outside the world of television, that world will become so entrenched as to render us powerless to do anything about it. Such a standing outside requires a religious perspective.

Several commentators on American religion have pointed out that American Protestantism is divided into two basic camps. In the 1960s Martin Marty called it the "two-party system" of conflicting ideologies:

One party, which may be called "Private" Protestantism, seized that name "evangelical" which had characterized all Protestants early in the nineteenth century. It accentuated individual salvation out of the world, personal moral life congruent with the ideals of the saved, and fulfillment or its absence in the rewards or punishments in another world in a life to come. The second informal group, which can be called "Public" Protestantism, was public insofar as it was more exposed to the social order and the social destinies of men.[11]

A decade later, a study of Episcopal churches by Wade Clark Roof showed that church people tend to be divided into two groups: the "locals" who prefer to live in small communities, get their satisfaction from relating closely to families and to friends, and belong to local groups; and the "cosmopolitans" who prefer living in large cities, get their satisfaction from dealing with ideas and international issues, and belong to large state or nationwide organizations.[12] At about the same time, research on the United Presbyterian Church revealed that there were two general theological orientations within that denomination. "One is otherworldly, dualistic in its view of humanity, strong in literal Scriptural authority, quite pessimistic about society, and mostly concerned about person-to-God relationships. The other is this worldly, unitary in its view of humanity, less committed to broad Scriptural authority, relatively optimistic about society, and mostly concerned about ethical behavior. . . . The two-party split is behind much of the discord over church priorities."[13]

The problem with the world of television is that it attacks *both* of these groups in the churches. It erodes the cosmopolitan, this-worldly group by refusing to deal honestly with the issues of the world, instead filtering out much of the reality and trivializing the rest. It also erodes the locals, those who find satisfaction in face-to-face relationships, by seducing them away from those personal relationships and substituting for them an ever-growing fantasy life. With regard to both religious groups, television emphasizes an individualism which rejects *both* community roots and the world of ideas.

The Vision

In previous chapters we have suggested the things concerned citizens can do: create local television councils and community action to get stations to accept their public accountability; introduce media education courses in the schools; use community organizations to develop programs relating to community issues in the "narrowcast" media of cable TV, videocassettes, low-power TV, public-broadcasting facilities, and commercial side-band channels; utilize stockholder action and, under certain circumstances, boycott.

But none of this can happen until people begin to understand what television is doing to them. Ignazio Silone observed that during the 1930s the peasants in southern Italy accepted their lot, from hunger to facism, as if it were a fact of nature or the will of God. Americans today seem to assume that the deterioration of their quality of life is inevitable, a given part of existence, and that the only solution is to get as much security as possible before it is too late. They have tolerated a costly war in Vietnam, corruption at the highest levels of government, deterioration of their phone service, transportation, and food quality, and a debt which can only crush their children's hopes for the future.

But this peasant-like passivity can end if people catch the vision of what our nation should be. Unfortunately, such a vision is next to impossible so long as the world of television limits our horizons by substituting its own pernicious vision of who we are and what we can become.

The Christian understanding of human nature recognizes the reality factor that impedes justice, namely, the self-interest deeply ingrained in every person which Christians call original sin. The persistence and perversity of human egoism is something that cannot be educated away, and it finds enormous power when multiplied through the structures of society. Gabriel Fackre has pointed out that relative justice is achievable only insofar as defensive power sets limits to offending power. This requires building checks and balances within the social system, and also generating centers of countervailing power in the form of public protest, citizen action, and even nonviolent civil disobedience.[14]

The problem is that television is supplying us with so many messages that we are able to pick and choose only those which reinforce our own individual biases; this encourages increasing opportunities to shut ourselves off from the rest of the world. This proliferation of choice effectively attenuates all outside and differing views. "Just me and my TV" gives us the impression of freedom. But it is a freedom without perspective, with no value center other than ourselves. Augustine showed us that freedom is not unlimited choice but increased self-control, a lesson which runs completely counter to the environment of television.

This is why community becomes so important: it can supply the "outside" reference point which can help extract persons from the addiction of quiet withdrawal into the world of TV. It can supply the "outside" reference point which helps relate people once again to the real world. Becoming involved in community is the best antidote to the dehumanizing experience which is a hallmark of TV-induced withdrawal.

So long as we accept the definition of the good for society in material and utilitarian terms proposed by the world of television, we are caught in what Hazel Henderson calls "the entropy trap"; that is, those material things which we value become ever more costly, and our expectations ever higher, to the point where no one any longer can afford to have what they *want*. But if we reject the materialist, utilitarian vision and instead define our goals in terms of human values, then we are freed from the entropy trap and can create alternative futures to improve our quality of life.

I have proposed an ethical perspective that goes beyond current legal requirements and national policies. In doing so, I have suggested that without a truly open marketplace of ideas, without a mass media environment in which all sides of issues are freely and openly discussed, we cannot have a workable democracy. Nor can we have what we in America call freedom—political or religious. For this reason, we have examined the issues of censorship, regulation, and the First Amendment protections from a perspective which asks what is right, just, and equitable, not simply what is currently legal or established public policy.

A note of caution here. If Christians and others with religious concern expect to contribute to this redefinition of goals and values, then they will have to go beyond expressing those goals and values in terms of the traditional forms of provincial and protected truths. When the church enters the world, its messages must increasingly be tested against the *general criteria*. It no longer can engage in "church" talk. What it is able to provide in the way of meaning in general human terms will be intelligible; the rest will not.

A friend of mine in Germany, a broadcaster of religious programs, once commented rather plaintively, "Is it asking too much when one asks the parson just for once, just once, to talk as a normal man to normal men, brief and to the point, without mincing matters, in a natural tone of voice, almost as in a friendly conversation?" This is the task of the whole church: to address the world in a natural tone of voice, almost as in a friendly conversation.

Communicating clearly and simply is especially important as the church attempts to converse with the men and women at work in the broadcasting industry. These people are no more a part of the problem than we ourselves. They, *and we,* are caught up in the system of television, of television-as-process. We must all come to this medium with a real love for it, while at the same time recognizing the distortions that come from its mythology. Our task is to create those structural changes which will allow television, and that means the people working in it, to reflect ourselves and our goals, rather than The Technique and its goal.

There is no reason why laws and regulation cannot assist in humanizing the system of television. We create traffic signals, speed limits, food regulations, health inspections, and other restraints on our freedom in order to maintain values of health and safety. Laws and regulations can also help maintain our value of an open marketplace of ideas—an opportunity to know what is going on in our community, nation, and world, to have access to our elected representatives, to enjoy a wide diversity of entertainment—all without endangering the value of free expression unfettered by government censorship.

History does not move simply because some new forms of technology arrive on the scene. History moves in response to human vision and activity. For us, it must start with the vision of a peaceful world, where gradually the production and distribution of armaments gives way to the production and distribution of goods and services that benefit the human race instead of threatening to destroy it, a vision of the rule of law rather than of economic domination, a vision of democracy where people are able to have a real say in what their own future will be, a vision of smallness and community involvement, a vision of cultural pluralism and a diversity of ideas, a vision of leisure spent meeting human needs.

If these ideals fail to materialize and find expression in our television and other mass communication, then Bellah's scenario of the rise of any one of a number of authoritarian systems becomes a serious alternative. At the present time, we are seeing a number of authoritarian expressions born of the frustrations people feel about the unjust and incomprehensible world in which we live. If these expressions continue to grow, and find resonance in mass media, the result could be a return to a world of even greater racial and religious bigotry, hatred, and political conflict.

Every culture has its own myths, and the content of those myths can encourage an open, mature, and peaceful coexistence, or a closed, self-centered existence of bias and conflict. The modern political myths which we see nightly on TV are just as powerful as the myths of any century. Supremacy of the "master race" in Germany, the "white man's burden" in Africa and Asia, the "manifest destiny" of settlers over the Indians in America, the "evil empire" of the Soviet Union—these and other myths are powerfully motivating and support various public policies and actions today.

The myths in American television do not create an environment conducive to growth, maturity, and freedom. This is why American television must be reconstructed, and the leadership in that reconstruction must come in part from the religious institutions of the nation. The Christian faith has an important contribution to make toward that reconstruction. Its views are not the views of the nation, but its "public religion" has been a major force in motivating and giving cohesion to the American experience for more than 200 years. As Martin Marty has said, the Christian faith does not belong in all its essentials to the consensus. The consensus represents the "proper" opinion whereas the Christian faith in its departure from the consensus, represents an "improper" opinion.[15]

The Christian strategy must be not only to express its "improper" opinion in the mass media, but also to make these media "mass." This means that the one-way, top-down, authoritarian qualities of the media must be refashioned in ways to make them two-way, people-to-people, and democratic. I have suggested some of the ways this can be done: increasing the number of TV networks to 6 or even 12; diversifying the sources of production; increasing support of public broadcasting and community-supported stations; the use of telephone call-ins; follow-up programs with discussions; community-media projects; more use of cable, videocassettes, and other less "mass" forms of the technology.

Churches must help other groups in society which are pressing for these new kinds of "small media." Fortunately, the church will find considerable common cause with many community organizations. For example, there is a real connection between media reform and the ecology movement today. Both are concerned with environmental deterioration, with the attitude that scorns future consequences of today's selfishness, with the failings of the technocratic world and instrumental values, with the disaster that follows treating everything as a commodity and people as things. Both hold a sacramental view that emphasizes the need to take care of all people, and that, with Whitehead, "God is not *before* all creation, but *with* all creation."[16]

It is one of the more hopeful signs that there are many groups and organizations today that share the church's concern about the technological era and its consequences. One of the church's main objectives must be to join in coalitions with such groups wherever they have common cause.

There is also hope, and considerable evidence, that we may have underestimated the continuing influence of those traditional institutions which have managed to survive without the benefit of the mass media for many years and which continue to transfer cultural values—the family, home, community, school, church, fraternal organizations, and others. These institutions have resisted attack before, and in recent years, some of them seem to be reasserting their role as conveyors of the stories which bridge the generation gap and tell us again who we are and what we might become.

The Christian faith does not promise success or even improvement, but it urges the faithful onward in hope. And, while we have no real reason to believe that the world of television can be completely turned around, at the same time those committed to the task of trying to do so continue to hold up in their communities of faith the ideals of open and free communication and a civility in our culture which we do not yet possess.

If religion cannot move with power and authority to bring about the changes necessary, it can at least whisper subversion and at the same time hold the vision high for those able to see it.

NOTES

Chapter 1: The World of Television

1. *Television: 1986 Nielsen Report* (Northbrook, Ill.: A. C. Nielsen Company, 1986), pp. 6-8.
2. Joan Gantz Cooney, "The Long Way to Go in Children's Television," *Broadcasting,* 13 October 1986, p. 26.
3. Mark Fetler, "Television Viewing and School Achievement," *Journal of Communication* 34/2 (Spring 1984): 104-118.
4. Daniel B. Wackmam, Ellen Wartella, and Scott Ward, "Learning to be Consumers: The Role of the Family," *Journal of Communication* 27/1 (Winter 1977): 118-124.
5. *Broadcasting/Cable Yearbook* (Washington, D.C.: Broadcasting Publications, 1986), p. A-2.5.
6. Burns W. Roper, "Trends in Attitudes toward Television and Other Media: A Twenty-Four Year Review," a report by The Roper Organization Inc. (New York: Television Information Office), 1983.
7. Alex S. Jones, "The Anchors, Who They Are, What They Do, the Tests They Face," *The New York Times Magazine,* 27 July 1986, p. 12.
8. The concept of media as the cultivator of culture was first proposed by George Gerbner in articles and reports during the 1960s in connection with his media research at the Annenberg School of Communication.
9. James Carey, "Communication and Culture," *Communication Research,* April 1975, pp. 173-191.
10. Ibid., p. 188.
11. Donald E. Miller, "The Future of Liberal Christianity," *The Christian Century,* 19 March 1982, p. 266.
12. Robert Bellah and Phillip E. Hammond, *Varieties of Civil Religion* (New York: Harper and Row, 1980), p. 16.
13. Emile Durkheim, *Elementary Forms of Religious Life,* trans. Joseph Swain (New York: Collier, 1961) [originally published in French, 1912], p. 62.
14. Paul Tillich, *The Interpretation of History* (New York: Scribner, 1936), p. 236.

Chapter 2: The Technological Era's Threat to Religion

1. Arend van Leewen, *Christianity in World History* (Edinburgh: Edinburgh Press, 1964).
2. Harvey Cox, *The Secular City* (New York: Macmillan, 1965).
3. Jacques Ellul, *The Technological Society* (New York: Knopf, 1967).
4. Neil Postman, *Amusing Ourselves to Death* (New York: Viking, 1984), p. 155.
5. Ibid., p. 110.

6. Cf. Paul Tillich, *The Protestant Era* (Chicago: University of Chicago Press, 1948).
7. H. Richard Niebuhr, *Christ and Culture* (New York: Harper, 1951).
8. Robert Bellah, et al., *Habits of the Heart* (Berkeley: University of California Press, 1985).

Chapter 3: A Theology of Communication

1. Avery Dulles, "The Church and the Media," *Catholic Mind*, 69/1256 (October 1971): 6-16.
2. *Websters New International Dictionary* (Springfield: Merriam, 1963), p. 460.
3. Philip H. Phenix, *Intelligible Religion* (New York: Harper, 1954).
4. Dulles, "The Church and the Media."
5. Knud Jorgensen, "God's Incarnation: the Centre of Communication," *Media Development* 27 (1981): 27-30.
6. Johannes Heinrichs, "Theory of Practical Communication: A Christian Approach," *Media Development* 27 (1981): 3-9.
7. Dorothy M. Emmet, *The Nature of Metaphysical Thinking* (London: Macmillan, 1953), p. 66.
8. John Cobb and David Griffin, *Process Theology* (Philadelphia: Westminster, 1976), p. 82.
9. Alfred N. Whitehead, *Modes of Thought* (New York: Macmillan, 1938), p. 57.
10. Walter J. Ong, *Orality and Literacy: The Technologizing of the Word* (New York: Methuen, 1982).
11. Harold Innis, *The Bias of Communication* (Toronto: University of Toronto Press, 1964).
12. Edmund Carpenter and Marshall McLuhan, *Explorations in Communication* (Boston: Beacon, 1960).
13. Melvin de Fleur, *Theories of Mass Communication* (New York: David McKay, 1975).
14. Martin Marty, *The Improper Opinion: Mass Media and the Christian Faith* (Philadelphia: Westminster, 1967).
15. Heinrichs, "Theory of Practical Communication,"
16. Dulles, "The Church and the Media."
17. Heinrichs, "Theory of Practical Communication," p. 7.
18. Ibid.
19. Paul Tillich, *Theology of Culture* (New York: Oxford University Press), chap. 15.
20. H. Richard Niebuhr, *The Meaning of Revelation* (New York: Macmillan, 1952), cf. especially pp. 43-90.
21. Robert N. Bellah, et al., *Habits of the Heart* (Berkeley: University of California Press, 1985).
22. Dulles, "The Church and the Media," p. 6.
23. Paul Tillich, *The Interpretation of History* (New York: Scribner, 1936), p. 236.
24. See Heinrichs, "Theory of Practical Communication," p. 7.
25. Ibid., p. 8.
26. Tillich, *Interpretation of History*, p. 48.
27. E. Schillebeeckx, "The Church and Mankind," *Concilium* 1 (Glen Rock, N.J.: Paulist, 1965), p. 88.
28. Gregory Baum, "Toward a New Catholic Theism," *The Ecumenicist* 8 (May-June 1970), p. 54.

29. Cf. Reinhold Niebuhr, *An Interpretation of Christian Ethics* (New York: Harper, 1935), and *The Nature and Destiny of Man,* vol. 1 (New York: Scribner, 1941).
30. Paul Tillich, *The Protestant Era* (Chicago: University of Chicago Press, 1948), pp. 200ff.; H. Richard Niebuhr, *The Meaning of Revelation* (New York: Macmillan, 1952), pp. 90ff., and *The Purpose of the Church and Its Ministry* (New York: Harper, 1956), pp. 42-75: Hendrik Kraemer, *The Communication of the Christian Faith* (Philadelphia: Westminster, 1956); Phenix, *Intelligible Religion;* Heinrichs, "Theory of Practical Communication," p. 8; and Dulles, "The Church and the Media."
31. Tillich, *The Protestant Era,* pp. 115-122.

Chapter 4: Television's Mythic World

1. Sherwood Schwartz, "Send Help before It's Too Late" *Parent's Choice,* Winter 1984, p. 2.
2. Cf. Jacques Ellul, *Propaganda* (New York: Knopf, 1965).
3. James Petersen, "Eyes Have They, but They See Not: A Conversation with Rudolf Arnheim," *Psychology Today,* June 1972, p. 55.
4. Abraham Moles, "A Skylight Open to the Neighborhood," *Intermedia* (International Broadcast Institute), February 1976, p. 6.
5. Michael R. Real, *Mass-Mediated Culture* (New York: Prentice-Hall, 1977), p. 6.
6. Stanley Kubrick, *Cultural Information Service,* January 1975, p. 12.
7. Cited from *Advertising Age,* 21 November 1973, p. 7.
8. Real, *Mass-Mediated Culture,* p. 48.
9. Gregor T. Goethals, *The TV Ritual: Worship at the Video Altar* (Boston: Beacon, 1981).
10. Joseph L. Price, "The Super Bowl as Religious Festival," *Christian Century,* 22 February 1984, pp. 190-191.
11. George Gerbner, address at International Communication Association, 21 April 1972.
12. Joyce Sprafkin, "Stereotypes on Television," monograph from Media Action Resource Center, 475 Riverside Drive, New York, NY 10115 (1975).
13. George Gerbner and Larry P. Gross, *Violence Profile No. 5,* University of Pennsylvania, June 1973.
14. Hannah Arendt, "Home to Roost: A Bicentennial Address," *New York Review,* 26 June 1975, p. 3.

Chapter 5: The Electronic Church and Its Message

1. "Stars of the Cathode Church," Time, 4 February 1980, pp. 64-65.
2. William F. McLoughlin, *Revivals, Awakenings, and Reform* (Chicago: University of Chicago Press, 1978), p. 10.
3. Ibid., pp. 12-13.
4. Anthony F. C. Wallace, "Revitalization Movements," *American Anthropology* 58 (1956): 264-281.
5. William F. Fore, "Religious Broadcasting," *International Encyclopedia of Communication* (New York: Oxford University Press, 1987).
6. *Congressional Record,* 73rd Congress, 2nd Session, vol. 78 (1934), Part 7, 7509.
7. Federal Communications Commission, *Communications Act of 1934* (Washington, D.C.: U.S. Government Printing Office, 1960), p. 40.

8. Federal Communications Commission, *Report of The F.C.C. to Congress pursuant to Section 307(c) of the Communications Act of 1934*, submitted from E. O. Sykes, Chairman to the President of the United States Senate, 22 January 1935, pp. 5-6.
9. Fore, "Religious Broadcasting."
10. *Greensboro News and Record* (Greensboro, N.C.), 1 June 1986, p. A12.
11. A. C. Nielsen, "Report on Devotional Programs, November 1986," *Nielsen Station Index* (New York: A. C. Nielsen, 1986).
12. Jeffrey K. Haddon and Charles Swann, *Prime Time Preachers: The Rising Power of Televangelism* (Reading, Mass.: Addison-Wesley, 1981), pp. 101-102.
13. Peter G. Horsfield, "And Now a Word from Our Sponsor: Religious Programs on American Television," *Review Francaise D'Etudes Americaines*, October 1981, 12:260-274. pp. 267-268.
14. Jerry Scholes, *Give Me That Prime-Time Religion: An Insider's Report on the Oral Roberts Evangelistic Association* (New York: Hawthorn, 1979), pp. 25-29.
15. Dick Dabney, "God's Own Network," *Harpers*, May 1980, p. 46.
16. Robert Bellah, *Varieties of Civil Religion* (New York: Harper, 1980), p. 107.
17. From a series of articles entitled "Heavenly Hosts" by staff writers Gerry Broome, Jack Chamberlain, Steve Haner, Sue Robinson, Cecile Holmes White, and Nan Wintersteller, in *Greensboro News and Record* (Greensboro, N.C.), June 1-4, 1986.
18. *Greensboro News and Record*, 1 June 1986, p. A13.
19. Ibid.
20. *Greensboro News and Record*, 2 June 1986, p. A6.
21. *Greensboro News and Record*, 3 June 1986, p. A6.
22. Ibid.
23. Ibid.
24. From a series of articles entitled "God among Us," by religion writer Carrie LaBriola and staff writer Vince McKelvey, in *Dayton Journal Herald* (Dayton, Ohio), November 19-26, 1981; 19 November 1981, p. 4.
25. Ibid.
26. Frances FitzGerald, "A Disciplined, Charging Army," *The New Yorker*, 18 May 1981, pp. 53-141.
27. *Dayton Journal Herald*, 17 November 1981, p. A6.
28. "PTL Counseling," leaflet published by the PTL Network, undated, cited in Peter G. Horsfield, *Religious Television: The American Experience* (New York: Longman, 1984), p. 57.
29. Peter G. Horsfield, "And Now a Word from Our Sponsor," p. 272.
30. *New York Times*, 21 March 1987, p. 1; ibid., 26 March 1987, p. A11.
31. *New York Times*, 26 March 1987, p. A16.
32. Ibid.
33. *New York Times*, 27 March 1987, p. A13.
34. *New York Times*, 26 March 1987, p. A16.
35. *Greensboro News and Record*, 2 June 1986, p. A6.
36. FitzGerald, "A Disciplined, Charging Army," pp. 135-138.
37. *Greensboro News and Record*, 1 June 1986, p. A12.
38. Robbie Gordon, "How They Tune Out the Press," *Washington Journalism Review*, April 1986, p. 43.

39. Ibid.

Chapter 6: The Electronic Church and Its Audience

1. George Gerbner, Larry Gross, Stewart Hoover, Michael Morgan, and Nancy Signorielli; and Harry E. Cotugno and Robert Wuthnow, "Religion and Television," a Research Report by the Annenberg School of Communications, University of Pennsylvania and the Gallup Organization, Inc., 2 vols. (New York: National Council of Churches, April 1984).
2. David Clark and Paul Virts, "Religious Television Audience: A New Development in Measuring Audience Size," paper presented at the Society for the Scientific Study of Religion, Savannah, 1985.
3. Stewart M. Hoover, George Gerbner, Larry Gross, Nancy Signorielli, and Michael Morgan, "The Religious Television Audience: A Matter of Significance, or Size?" (Philadelphia: Temple University, February 1986).
4. Ibid., p. 34.
5. Gerbner, vol. 1, pp. 2-3.
6. Ibid., vol. l, p. 52.
7. Ibid., vol. l, p. 10.
8. Ibid., vol. 1, p. 12.
9. Martin Marty, "The Explosion in Evangelical Television," *Laity Exchange*, a monograph of the Audenshaw Foundation (London: Audenshaw Foundation, 1978), p. 3.
10. Martin Marty, "The Invisible Religion," *Presbyterian Survey*, May 1979, p. 13.

Chapter 7: Strategies for Mainline Churches

1. H. Richard Niebuhr, *The Purpose of the Church and Its Ministry* (New York: Harper, 1956), p. 26.
2. Paul Tillich, *The Protestant Era* (Chicago: University of Chicago, 1948).
3. Paul O. Freire, *The Politics of Education: Culture, Power, and Liberation* (South Hadley, Mass.: Bergin and Gervey, 1985).
4. Tillich, *The Protestant Era*, p. 204.
5. Ibid., p. 219.
6. Russ Read, "The Church and the Media: A Strategy for Outreach," in *Church Growth: America*, March-April, 1978.
7. Fred Friendly, in a speech delivered to the International Radio and Television Society, New York, N.Y., 1967.

Chapter 8: Media Violence Is Hazardous to Your Health

1. Jervis Anderson, "An Extraordinary People," *The New Yorker*, 12 November 1984, p. 128.
2. U.S. Department of Commerce, Bureau of the Census, *Statistical Abstract of the United States 1985* (Washington: U.S. Government Printing Office, 1984), pp. 166, 172, 183.
3. National Commission on the Causes and Prevention of Violence, "Commission Statement on Violence in Television Entertainment Programs," 23 September 1969 (Washington: U.S. Government Printing Office).

4. Ibid., p. 7.
5. *Broadcasting* magazine, 27 March 1972, p. 25.
6. David M. Blank, "The Gerbner Violence Profile," in *Journal of Broadcasting* 21/3 (Summer 1977): 273-279.
7. George Gerbner, Larry Gross, Michael F. Eleey, Marilyn Jackson-Beeck, Suzanne Jeffries-Fox, and Nancy Signorielli, "The Gerbner Violence Profile: An Analysis of the CBS Report," *Journal of Broadcasting* 21/3 (Summer 1977): 280-286.
8. "Social/Behavioral Effects of Violence on Television," Hearing before the Subcommittee on Telecommunications, Consumer Protection, and Finance of the Committee on Energy and Commerce, House of Representatives Ninety-Seventh Congress, First Session, October 21, 1981 (Washington: U.S. Government Printing Office), Serial No. 97-84, p. 127.
9. "Research on Television Violence: The Fact of Dissent." CBS memorandum October 21, 1981, quoted in William Fore, "Media Violence: Hazardous to Our Health," *Christian Century,* 25 September 1985, p. 835.
10. National Institute of Mental Health, "Television and Behavior: Ten Years of Scientific Progress and Implications for the Eighties," NIMH, Washington, D.C. 1982, p. 6.
11. Ibid.
12. Thomas D. Cook, Deborah A. Kendzierski, and Stephen V. Thomas, "The Implicit Assumptions of Television Research: An Analysis of the 1982 NIMH Report on Television and Behavior," *Public Opinion Quarterly,* Summer 1983, p. 198.
13. This and all following quotations, unless otherwise noted, are from "Violence and Sexual Violence in Film, Television, Cable and Home Video," a report of a study committee of the Communication Commission, National Council of the Churches of Christ in the U.S.A., New York, 1985.
14. David Pearl, "Television: Behavioral and Attitudinal Influences," National Institute of Mental Health, Washington, D.C. (1985), p. 6.
15. George Gerbner, "Gratuitous Violence and Exploitative Sex: What Are the Lessons? (Including Violence Profile No. 13)," prepared for the Study Committee of the Communications Commission of the National Council of the Churches of Christ in the U.S.A., 21 September 1984 (Annenberg School of Communications, University of Pennsylvania, Philadelphia PA 19104), pp. 2-3.
16. Ibid., pp. 5-6.
17. Ibid., pp. 10-11.
18. Ibid., p. 20.
19. NCC, "Violence and Sexual Violence," p. 8.
20. Ibid., p. 8.
21. J. Ronald Milavsky, "Sex, Violence and the Media," a paper presented to the Study Committee of the Communication Commission of the National Council of the Churches of Christ in the U.S.A., 21 September 1984 (National Broadcasting Company, New York).
22. Ibid., p. 16.
23. NCC, "Violence and Sexual Violence," p. 9.
24. Ibid., p. 9.

Chapter 9: What We Can Do about Media Violence

1. All references in Chapter 9 are from "Violence and Sexual Violence in Film, Television, Cable and Home Video," a report of a Study Committee of the Communication Commission, National Council of the Churches of Christ in the U.S.A., New York, 1985.
2. "Violence and Sexual Violence," p. 10.
3. Ibid.
4. Ibid., pp. 10-11.
5. Ibid., p. 11.
6. Ibid.
7. Ibid.
8. Ibid., p. 12.
9. Ibid.
10. Ibid.
11. Ibid.
12. Ibid.

Chapter 10: How to Bust the Communication Trust

1. Ronald A. Cass, *Revolution in the Wasteland* (Charlottesville: University Press of Virginia, 1981), p. 61.
2. Ibid., p. 13.
3. Ibid., p. 45.
4. Ibid., p. 69.
5. Ibid., p. 53.
6. Eric Barnouw, *The Image Empire* (New York: Oxford University Press, 1970), p. 335.
7. "New York Report: NBC Says It Will Show Film on Jesus Despite Opposition," *TV Guide*, 2 April 1977, p. A-3.
8. Anne W. Branscomb, "An Outsider Looking into the Poverty of Public Broadcasting," address at the National Association of Educational Broadcasters, 14 November 1977.
9. Anne W. Branscomb and Maria Savage, "The Broadcast Reform Movement: At the Crossroads," *Journal of Communication* 28/4 (1978): 30-31.
10. Ibid., p. 34.
11. "The Public Trust," The Carnegie Commission on the Future of Public Broadcasting (1979), p. 21.

Chapter 11: U.S. Media: The Whole World Is Watching

1. "Universal Declaration of Human Rights," 10 December 1948 (New York: United Nations Department of Publication), p. 6.
2. "The Global First Amendment War," *Time*, 6 October 1980, p. 63.
3. *Report on a New World Communication Order*, International Commission for the Study of Communication Problems (the MacBride Commission) (New York: UNESCO, 1980).
4. Ronald Dworkin, "Is the Press Losing the First Amendment?" *New York Review of Books*, 4 December 1980, p. 49. Emphasis added.

5. Red Lion Broadcasting Co. v. Federal Communications Commission, 395 U.S. 367 (1969).
6. Howard C. Anawalt, "Is the MacBride Commission's Approach Compatible with the United States Constitution?" *Journal of Communication*, Autumn 1981, p. 128.
7. Frank Campbell in "Debate Sharpens on New World Information Order," *New York Times*, 15 February 1981, Sec. 4, p. E3.
8. Ibid.
9. *Report on a New World Communication Order.*

Chapter 12: Signs of Hope

1. Joseph T. Klapper and Otter Kilenberg, "The Mass Media: Their Impact on Children and Family Life," remarks to the Child Study Association of America, 21 March 1960; distributed by the Television Information Office, New York.
2. William Kuhns, *The Electronic Gospel* (New York: Herder and Herder, 1969), p. 165.
3. Ibid., p. 166.
4. Avery Dulles, "The Church Is Communications," U.S. Catholic Conference Documentary Service, 20 April 1971 (New York: U.S. Catholic Conference).
5. Ibid., p. 8.
6. Robert Bellah, *Varieties of Civil Religion* (New York: Harper and Row, 1980), pp. 8-17.
7. Ibid., p. 185.
8. Ibid., p. 16.
9. Alexis de Tocqueville, *Democracy in America,* trans. George Lawrence (New York: Doubleday, 1967), p. 508.
10. Bellah, *Varieties of Civil Religion,* p. 20.
11. Martin Marty, *Righteous Empire: The Protestant Experience in America* (New York: Dial, 1970), p. 179.
12. Wade Clark Roof, *Community and Commitment: Religious Plausibility in a Liberal Protestant Church* (New York: Elsevier, 1984).
13. Dean R. Hoge, Everett L. Perry, and Gerald L. Klever, "Theology as a Source of Disagreement about Protestant Church Goals and Priorities," *Review of Religious Research,* 19/2 (Winter 1978): p. 116.
14. Gabriel Fackre, "Archie Bunker: Visions and Realities," *The Christian Century,* 19 July 1972, p. 773.
15. Martin Marty, *The Improper Opinion: Mass Media and the Christian Faith* (Philadelphia: Westminster, 1967).
16. A. N. Whitehead, *Process and Reality* (New York: Macmillan, 1929), p. 521.

INDEX

214